DEPARTMENT OF DEGENERATES

A HUMOROUS & RAUCOUS MILITARY MEMOIR

ALEXANDER LEE

Copyright © 2024 ALEXANDER LEE

All rights reserved. No part of this publication may be reproduced, distributed, or transmitted in any form or by any means, including photocopying, recording, or other electronic or mechanical methods, without the prior written permission of the publisher, except in the case of brief quotations embodied in critical reviews and certain other noncommercial uses permitted by copyright law.

DISCLAIMER:
The views expressed in this publication are those of the author and do not necessarily reflect the official policy or position of the Department of Defense or the U.S. government. The public release clearance of this publication by the Department of Defense does not imply Department of Defense endorsement or factual accuracy of the material.

This book, titled "Department of Degenerates," is a work of satire. It is not endorsed, sanctioned, or supported by the Department of Defense, Department of the Army or any other government agency. The stories within are based on true events but have been modified for satirical purposes and to protect individuals' privacy. Names, characters, businesses, places, events, locales, and incidents are either products of the author's imagination or used fictitiously. Any resemblance to actual persons, living or dead, or actual events is purely coincidental.

While the author has military experience, the experiences recounted herein are fictionalized and embellished for satire. "Specialist Joe" is a fictional composite character created for storytelling purposes. The character's experiences, opinions, and actions should not be associated with any real person. The views expressed in this book are those of the author's satirical persona and do not reflect official policy or position.

The strategies, tactics, and procedures mentioned are not intended as reflections of actual practices nor as recommendations. The author assumes no responsibility or liability for any errors or omissions in the content of this book, nor for any actions taken based on its content. This book is provided on an "as is" basis and is intended for entertainment and thought-provoking purposes on military life. It is not a guide, historical account, or documentary of actual events.

ISBN: 978-1-7373634-2-2

For all questions and comments, please contact:
MindGameManuscripts@gmail.com

Book design by Maureen Cutajar
www.gopublished.com

To enlisted folks,

This book is dedicated to all the enlisted.
All of you underpaid, disgruntled, half-assers. I hope (and fear) that many of you will relate well to these stories. Keep your head down, keep chumming along, and keep making memories.

I love ya even if your platoon daddy doesn't.

CONTENTS

PART 1: SHIT STORIES

It Depends 3
Delta Defecation 12
Hiroshima Ain't Got Nothing On Me 20
RLTW 27
Thrilla in Manila 35

PART 2: BARRACKS BUNNIES AND STRIPPERS

The Science of Barracks Bunnies 43
Blue Balls and Green Weenies 45
Fayettenam's Finest 52
Bailing and Railing 64
Unsolicited Rant About The 82nd Airborne 76
The Cock Block 79
Mrs. Right 83
PEP in My Step 91
Random Text Message from Joe 96

PART 3: MEDICAL MISHAPS

The Dick Bomb 101
Dirty Dancing 111
Bursting My Bursa 115

PART 4: THE DERRIERE DIARY

Preface to The Derriere Diary 121
My Third Butt Cheek: Part One 122
My Third Butt Cheek: Part Two 129
My Third Butt Cheek: Part Three 140
Death Shit 148

PART 5: WEIRD-ASS ROOMMATES

My Weird Roommate #1: Spiderman 159
My Weird Roommate #2: Choirboy 167

PART 6: RANDOM ACTS OF DEGENERACY

Burning Man 179
Goat Fucker 184
SOF vs LARPERS 192
A Bubble Bath 198
RAWR 203

About the Author 213

AUTHOR'S NOTE

My name is Specialist Joe. I am a former paratrooper and special operations soldier. This is a collection of the most ridiculous and depraved stories from my service. These are not your typical war stories. If you're looking for a cool guy telling heroic cool-guy stories (looking at you, SEALs), then this book is not for you.

This is not a circle jerk. I'm not looking for kudos or attaboys. I'm more of a hedonistic anti-hero—maybe even an asshole idiot—and you will probably think less of me after reading this.

So here are the depraved tales from the Department of Degenerates.

PART 1
SHIT STORIES

IT DEPENDS

This story occurred shortly after basic training when I was at Fort Benning—where it's hot as fuck—in my last week of Airborne School, a school where you jump out of planes and learn to be a paratrooper. To graduate, we had to complete five jumps. The issue was that they would keep us rigged up in our chutes for eight hours or longer waiting to get the "all clear." During this waiting period, there was nowhere to pee, so most guys would sit around not drinking water. Subsequently, many guys would become dehydrated as they sat inside the sweltering riggers shed. I'd already seen a few dudes go down as heat casualties.

The choice we faced was simple: suffer dehydration, or potentially piss your pants and become the laughingstock of Airborne School. 99.999% of soldiers chose the first option. I was in a tough situation, with conditions I deemed unacceptable. "Not me," I'd decided before my first jump. I was the 0.001% who went the other way, expanded my mind, and came up with an alternative.

The other soldiers already thought I was a little "off." Of course, I knew that the scheme I was embarking on would solidify this sentiment. I'd already learned that this was the price of genius—
the untold burden carried by those on the cutting edge. Innovation and insanity have the same number of syllables, after all. But then again, so does idiocy. I was, however, committed to the plan, and I had to see it through.

I was standing in aisle nine at the PX when I had my eureka moment. I spotted an 88-pack of extra-absorbent Depends. Sold!

That package ended up stuffed into my barracks wall locker. Literally stuffed. It was quite a sizable bundle and I had to really put my shoulder into it to get the locker shut. A sense of smug satisfaction enveloped me, knowing I had ingeniously outwitted the game. I shared the good news with my chalk mates (guys I jump out of planes with), explaining the myriad of benefits an adult diaper could provide to would-be paratroopers. Generously, I offered them a good deal—a mere three bucks a diaper. But my diaper evangelism fell upon deaf ears. I'd been convinced they were going to sell like hotcakes, but it seemed that my counterparts would need some convincing.

Greg, whose locker stood next to mine, slipped me a sideways look.

"What?" I asked.

"No one wants to wear a diaper, you idiot."

"Why wouldn't they?"

"Why would they?" he asked, probably thinking rhetorically.

"Because once the Jumpmasters put on your parachute and do their checks, you can't take the thing off. We might be sitting rigged up in that damn shed for who knows how long. Guys from the last class told me they had to sit around in 102 degree heat for over twelve hours before the winds were good for a jump. Twelve hours, Greg, without peeing! The next day the poor bastards just decided not to drink anything, and it was nearly 100 degrees in that room. Some of them passed out and had to get recycled. Guys were passing out on the landing zone… that's why the diaper!"

I shook my Depends at Greg and watched him process my logic. It was irrefutable. Bulletproof. I saw my profound wisdom slowly dawn on him. He started to shake his head.

"Nah, I'm gonna pass, man."

"Why?"

"Because I don't want to wear a fucking diaper. Have some dignity, man."

"Dignity? Dignity! Greg, didn't you just bang Airborne Shirley?"

He frowned at me, looking from side to side. "You keep your mouth shut!" he said.

I laughed. "Come on, Greg, she posted it on her Snapchat—we saw you balls deep in that hog. Not to mention she'd just dropped off a trio before picking your ass up," I said. Greg's face reddened. Airborne Shirley was an obese local, known to park her van right next to the barracks and pick up random dudes and bang them. She would come multiple times a day—pun intended.

"Let's see how it goes for you first," Greg said, then walked off.

"Really, Greg? You'll shove your cock into that fat slut but not into a pair of unadulterated Depends?" I yelled after him. "Pride goeth before the fall," I chuckled.

(The next day)

Wearing a parachute, I awkwardly shuffled over to where the jumpmaster stood, waiting for me to approach him. "Move it, specialist, I don't have all day!"

I shuffled faster, my Depends rubbing up against my cargo pants and making a whishing sound. The jumpmaster double-checked my leg straps. The sound was throwing him off. He checked my harnesses, parachute, and reserve, turned me around, and slapped me on the ass (as they do). The diaper crinkled and I felt his eyes on me as I waddled back over to the wooden bench and sat down next to Greg.

"Well," he said, "Have you used it yet?"

"No. We've only been in here for thirty minutes."

(1 hour later)

My chalk mates were sweating profusely. I moved over to the Gatorade beverage cooler for my third cup. I came back to Greg, who was looking at me with disgust. The guy to my left, who had no idea that I was wearing a diaper, said, "You're gonna have to pee, man."

"Oh, I know," I said as I threw back the Gatorade.

(1 hour later)

I was still sweating effectively, but some guys had already stopped. The guy to my left just wouldn't shut the fuck up and my bladder felt like it was going to explode. And to be honest, I wasn't completely sure that the Depends would hold up. I hadn't given them a test drive, breaking one of the Army's most sacred rules: "Always test your equipment." My worst fear was that I'd pee too much and it'd leak and soil my pants or worse yet, run down the bench onto the others. But I had already crossed the Rubicon, so I would do it live. First, I let out a slight tinkle, then cut it off. Then waited... I definitely felt a little pee on my skin, but it felt like the diaper was absorbing most of it. Since all seemed good, I released my first torrent of piss. I leaned my head back and let out a sigh.

"You're fucking peeing, aren't you?" said Greg.

"Yup," I said. The guy to my left squirmed away from me, and those in my vicinity were now disgusted, but Greg and I laughed.

(2 hours later)

The guy to my left started complaining that he had to pee badly and was worried he was going to piss his pants.

"You should do it," I said, then downed my 10th cup of Gatorade in front of him, which at that point had just become a huge flex and a testimony to the power of Depends Ultra Absorbent.

(2 hours later)

I felt like a genius. The thing I'd worried about with the diaper was whether peeing in the same spot repeatedly would cause me to spring a leak. I'd done some research and thinking though, and I'd decided to tuck my pecker as far back between my legs as I could go, so that I would pee towards the back of the diaper. My theory was that as I peed, the diaper in that surrounding area would get wet and cool and subsequently, my penis would cool and retract towards my body, automatically adjusting my point of aim to the front of my diaper.

Marvelously, I was correct. My plan went precisely as planned. I proceeded to explain my now proven hypothesis to the guys immediately near me.

(2 hours later)

I took one last tinkle for good measure before standing up in line to board the aircraft. By this point, everyone was complaining about how badly they had to pee. Some complained of nausea and dizziness. Greg himself was squirming a little. Not me.

"First thing I'm gonna do when I land is rollover, whip my dick out, and pee," he said.

"Hey man, I've peed like six times already. If you want a Depends, hit me up later."

"You know... I actually might," Greg said.

One client—perfect. I could now charge a premium, get my money back on the purchase, and potentially turn a profit. I never felt as smug as I did at that particular moment. I couldn't wait to tell everyone "I told you so" later on in the barracks.

(30 minutes later)

"Outboard personnel, stand up!" The jumpmaster yelled, and we awkwardly stood up in our bulky parachutes. Rookie paratroopers nervously jostling each other in the back of the cramped C-130. I saw the jumpmasters between the rows of guys; they made a weird pumping motion. "Hook up!" they bellowed, then we echoed. All the jumpers on the stick connected their static lines to the cable that ran along the plane—which is super critical, by the way, otherwise your parachute wouldn't deploy, and you'd most likely die. I'd been told that the reserve was there mostly to make us feel better about jumping out of a plane. I tried hard not to think about this.

"Sound off for equipment check," the jumpmasters sounded ahead of us. One by one, down the line, each man in the stick inspected the connection to the anchoring of the man in front of him, then the line, then the fit of their harness. As is the procedure, once you'd verified that your buddy's shit was in order, you slapped his ass, then he did the same thing to the guy in front of him. Greg was behind me.

"You're crazy if you think I'm touching your shit," Greg said from behind me. He was being a sissy and didn't want to check my leg straps.

"Make sure you check the straps around the diaper. I'd hate for it to fall off when my chute deploys," I said.

"Okay!" he yelled as he gave my ass the customary slap. I felt a slight wet squish as he did so. Then I checked the guy in front of me and slapped his ass as well, and so on.

"Okay!" Butt slap!

Pretty soon we got the green light, and the first-time parachutists began exiting the bird.

I airborne shuffled toward the jump door. Seeing screaming men launch themselves and get ripped out of the plane by the wind, and knowing that I was next, was making my butt pucker. The only bright side being that if I shit myself, the Depends had me covered. Then it was my turn.

I passed my line to the jumpmaster, executed a ninety-degree turn, and stared out into the rushing void. Then I jumped.

I kicked out my leg, vaulted out of the plane, and counted to six.

"One thousand." The wind ripped at me.

"Two thousand." I felt the static line tighten and pull out of the chute.

"Three thousand." Holy shit! I'm fucking falling!

"Four thousand." Why am I still falling?

"Five thousand." The parachute caught air and jerked me up. My harness tightened around me.

"Six thousand." The cool, damp diaper pressed up against my skin, and fuck! I was paratrooping for the first time. Reflexively I went through the steps in my training. "Check canopy and gain canopy control," I remembered. They had drilled it deep into my skull over the last three weeks.

Looking up and seeing that my risers were twisted all around, I pulled them apart and pedaled my legs like there was an invisible bicycle. The earth beneath me spun as the risers untwisted until the last twist came undone and I was floating down to earth.

I laughed and let out a hoot. The other jumpers around me fell at a similar rate, which was a good thing—it meant that I wasn't falling too fast. The ground beneath me moved from my left to right, which meant that I needed to grab a right-side riser to stop the drift. I reached up and pulled down, and it seemed to do very little.

"Fucking airborne pricks told me this would brake the parachute... what the fuck!" Why was I going faster? The ground approached and I rehearsed what I would do. I needed to prepare to execute a Parachute Landing Fall otherwise known as a PLF. I'd done these so many times but never on an actual jump. Judging by how fast the ground was moving by, I was burning in. I put my feet and knees together, planning to let the balls of my feet hit, then bend my knees, striking my calf, butt, and then side, which would turn into a flawlessly executed PLF.

It didn't matter—the training was all bullshit. As I slammed my feet and then my ass, something hot and wet shot down my leg. Then the parachute caught some wind and dragged me across the drop zone. I was a bit woozy, having suffered a minor concussion. I was struggling to flip open my two canopy release assemblies. I felt a sharp pain in my leg and warmth. Shit, was that my guts? I got one then two, and the parachute detached, and I slid to a halt on the dusty ground. I'd landed in the middle of a dirt road on the drop zone. It was the hardest spot possible. I laid there on my back for a while, groaning, with the wind knocked out of me.

After recovering I sat upright and felt around my arms, then my legs to see if anything was broken. I felt the wetness down the back and front of my legs, and I worried that I was bleeding, I pressed my hands to my pants and lifted them. I realized that it wasn't blood.

I'd just pissed myself.

I smelled my hands to be certain. "Oh fuck!" I said aloud, realizing that my piss was all over me. "Fuck!" I said again, realizing that I had to walk back to the collection point in front of everyone, including my airborne instructors. Then, as I felt around, I realized that the impact had wrung the backside of my diaper like a fucking sponge. I'd had twelve Gatorades worth of old piss shoot down my leg. It was somehow worse than fresh piss.

I hadn't expected this, so I reached down the front of my pants and tore the diaper off like I was Magic Mike ripping off a thong. I stood in the middle of the drop zone, paratroopers falling all around me holding out an adult diaper at arm's length with piss-soaked pants. Upon examination, it proved my suspicion; the diaper had been blown out and crushed in the back. Though on a positive note, it probably softened my landing.

I tossed the diaper onto the side of the road and started gathering up my parachute, all the while I tried to concoct some plausible story as to why I was wet and smelled like urine. I looked all around me for some kind of puddle that I could claim I had landed in. It would be better to show up muddy than piss soaked, but unfortunately, it hadn't rained.

(15 minutes later)

I arrived, panting and still soaked, at the gathering point. Everyone who had been on that jump stood in line in the order in which we'd jumped. A Black Hat (an instructor) took accountability. Greg came up behind me.

"Yo, what the fuck happ...?" His question trailed off as he sniffed the air. "No fucking way," he said.

"I landed in a puddle, Greg," I said.

Greg laughed behind me. He obviously didn't buy it for a second. The kid in front of me turned back, looked, then chuckled to himself; the Black Hat glanced up, checked my name tag, and continued down the line checking names off the clipboard. *Thank God he didn't notice*, I thought to myself. I was embarrassed enough. I knew once we got to the barracks, I'd become the laughingstock of Airborne School.

Just when things felt like they couldn't get any worse, another Black Hat approached carrying a stick, and at the end of the stick was a Depends Extra Absorbent diaper that looked like it'd been thrown out of a plane. Well, it had, but at the time it was still attached to me.

"Men, who littered my drop zone? Did I not explicitly say not to leave any trash on my drop zone, and here I find a fucking diaper!" He shook his stick at us menacingly. I swallowed a lump in my throat, then went stiff as a board when his eyes fixed on me. I heard that guy from Jurassic Park's voice in my head: *Don't move, it can't see us if we don't move*, but his wisdom failed me, and quickly I was spotted in my piss-soaked ACUs.

"Front leaning rest position... Move!"

"Goddamn it," someone said. Greg also cursed me under his breath. Now we all got smoked because I'd decided to litter the drop zone with a dirty diaper. And as we struggled under the hot Georgia sun, the heat and sweat amplified the stench of my piss-soaked clothes.

DELTA DEFECATION

This story occurred when I was a Special Forces candidate. We'd just finished an overnight detail near Camp Mackall, where we'd been tasked out with cleaning out Special Forces latrines—a very unpleasant task, as SF guys love their protein. When not unclogging toilets, the personnel assigned to this detail lodged at a remote cabin. The detail had finally come to an end, and Greg and I made the long drive back to Fort Bragg. I'd just gotten to my barracks room and was firing up the ol' Xbox, when someone knocked at my door. There stood Greg.

"Hey bro, I left my dog tags," Greg said.

"That fucking sucks…" I began to close the door in his face.

"You know what happens if I don't have my dog tags at formation tomorrow, right?" Greg interjected.

I stood with the door cracked and remembered the last time a fellow student had failed to have their dog tags at formation. It hadn't been pretty; they pushed our shit in for hours.

"Fuck, man! Let me get my shit." I shut the door in his face. I got my shit together and mentally prepared myself for the drive back to Camp Mackall.

On our way out of the barracks, we ran into another student, whom the class and cadre referred to as "Weirdo." Weirdo was a mountain of a man who had the mannerisms of a toddler and disproportionally large innocent looking eyes; he loved anime and talking about anime, and was possibly a touch autistic.

"Hey guys, what ya doing?" Weirdo asked.

"Greg forgot his dog tags. We're about to drive back to the cabin to get them," I said.

"Oh... can I come along?" Weirdo said. Greg and I looked at each other, confused.

"You know it's a forty-five minute drive out into the middle of nowhere and forty-five minutes back?" Greg said.

"I don't care. I'll tag along," Weirdo said. I shrugged my shoulders, and we went to the car.

It was a long and uneventful drive out to the cabin. Weirdo made awkward jokes and repeatedly tried to steer the conversation toward anime, which Greg and I could not relate to. Luckily Greg was able to secure his dog tags.

We had just left the cabin and were approaching a red light near one of the last gas stations for miles when I smelled something foul coming from the backseat. I looked in my rearview mirror and saw Weirdo making a face and sniffing around with a look of false suspicion.

"Alright... Who ripped ass?" I asked.

"Weirdo, was that you?" Greg said.

I could see Weirdo shaking his head in denial in the back seat.

"Nope, wasn't me... probably a skunk." His face turned a bit red, I assumed from embarrassment. He was an awful liar.

"Dude, do you need to use the restroom? This is the last gas station for a while," I said, though I genuinely did not care that he had farted.

Greg was laughing. "Well, whoever did that probably should

check their shorts," he said as he lowered his window. I laughed. It was a pretty bad fart.

"I'm fine, just keep going, I *don't* have to go," Weirdo said.

"Alrighty then," I said and continued into the middle of nowhere, heading towards home.

Greg and I got to talking and had the radio playing. Weirdo was silent in the back. About ten minutes after the first "alleged fart," another smell wafted forward, and it was potent. My eyes watered up, and we could not roll the windows down fast enough. I about swerved into oncoming traffic as I tried to get my head out the window.

"Jesus fucking Christ, dude, what the fuck did you eat?" Greg said.

I looked into the rearview mirror and saw that Weirdo's face had turned a dark red, a vein protruded from his forehead, and his eyes focused on something ahead of him. "Weirdo, you okay, buddy?" I asked.

He nodded his head in response.

"Like, bro, do you need to take a shit, man?" Greg asked, seeing that an exit was coming up.

"Hey, buddy, you want me to take the next exit and see if we can find you a bathroom?"

"I don't need to go!" Weirdo shouted. "Just keep *fucking* driving!"

Greg and I looked at each other in disbelief. So I heeded his request and kept driving.

Five minutes later another malodorous assault commenced. I looked into the rearview mirror once again, and Weirdo's face had turned a dark purple, the vein jutted from his forehead, and his body was trembling.

"Hey, man... I'm worried you're gonna shit in my car. How about I pull over somewhere?" I said.

He did not respond.

I turned to Greg. "Dude... do we need to take this guy to a hospital?"

Greg leaned back and said, "Hey, dude, do you just need to shit? Or what's wrong?"

Weirdo's eyes bulged from his head as he made eye contact with Greg. "I need to poop now!"

"Okay! Whelp, it looks like it's gonna have to be in the woods then," I said. I quickly pulled off onto a gravel road that led into the woods.

◆

I found a relatively clear spot in the woods, a back road that no one was going to be coming down. I put the car in park and told Weirdo that we'd wait here. Weirdo got out of the back of the car and walked into the woods straight behind our vehicle. He got behind a single tree maybe ten yards behind our vehicle, dropped his drawers, and took a fat shit. The reason I know this is that both Greg and I saw the entire thing go down. Behind a lone, thin pine tree, directly in line with our rear-view mirror, he stuck his ass out from behind the tree, giving us a clear view to witness the event.

"Bro, does he know we can see him?" I asked.

"I don't think so, I think because he can't see us, he thinks we can't see him," Greg said. We both started laughing. I looked and indeed, the only part of him that was obscured was his head.

"What a fucking moron," Greg said. I agreed.

While I'm not proud of this, Greg and I watched this man shit. At one point this long turd slithered out of Weirdo's ass and got stuck. He probably had a good nine inches hanging out of him, and we watched as Weirdo made an aggressive twerking motion as he tried to dislodge the turd. He had great difficulty. Greg and I began laughing hysterically. Eventually, he pinched it off.

"Guys! Do you have any toilet paper?" Weirdo yelled out, still squatting, his dirty ass very visible to both Greg and me. We were laughing so hard that we could barely breathe. We half-assedly looked around for something he could wipe with—napkins, Lysol wipes, anything.

"We got nothing, bro..." I yelled back.

"Oh okay... I got something," Weirdo said. We watched as, with his pants still down, he proceeded to remove a shoe, then a sock. Weirdo then threaded the sock between his legs and into his ass crack, then with a hand securing the sock both behind and in front of him, began to make a rapid shimmying motion with the sock.

"What the fuck is he doing?" Greg said, and we both began cackling again. A short time later, Weirdo got his pants back on and his boot, and came walking up to my window holding the clean end of the sock between two pinched fingers, like a child holding a worm.

"Hey, do you have a bag or something I can put this in?" He held his shit-covered sock proudly before me.

"Dude, throw that fucking thing into the woods!" I said. Weirdo glumly threw the sock into the woods behind us, like he was disappointed because he wanted to take it home and wash it or something, before getting back into the car. Greg and I looked at each other, trying to stifle our laughter.

"You good, bro?" I asked.

"Yeah, I'm good now," Weirdo said. Seeing as the color had returned to his face and that he had just dropped a considerable shit, I deemed us good to go.

I was wrong.

Fifteen minutes further down the road, another odiferous whiff propagated throughout the vehicle. I rolled down my window, almost hit a deer, then looked back at Weirdo. His face had once again turned purple.

We pulled off the road, not too far from Bragg. We passed some nearby places with fences and security. I didn't know exactly where we were. I parked the car and Weirdo hopped out and sprinted, thankfully deeper into the woods this time where we could not see him.

"Can you believe this guy?" Greg said.

"Yeah, I mean, I just wish he would have admitted to needing to poop. He could have used the toilet at the gas station. That's what I don't get about it," I said.

"Yeah—" He turned his head to the woods to our left and spotted something. "Hey Joe, I'm seeing a bunch of 'Do Not Trespass' signs. What do you think those are about?"

"I'm not sure. I've seen some fences and patrol vehicles in the area though. Some secret squirrel shit is out around here somewhere."

"Huh…" Greg said. We waited, uneventfully, for Weirdo to return.

Weirdo walked out of the woods very slowly, with his hands in the air. His eyes were wide as a deer in the headlights. He slowly reached for the car door and slid into the back.

"Yo, what's wrong bu—"

"Just drive, drive now!" Weirdo said. I looked at Greg, put the car in gear, and noticed headlights deep in the woods behind us.

"Yo… what the fuck happened out there?" Greg asked.

"Well, I was starting to poop, when suddenly a spotlight falls on me, and these vehicles roll up on me. I turn around and there are like six operator-looking dudes with guns at the ready. I was just squatting with a turd hanging from my ass."

"*What*?" I said.

"What the fuck did they tell you?" Greg asked.

"Not much. I just kinda looked at them, and they looked at me. I heard some radio chatter… and I pooped, then I came back here, and… we ought to leave now," Weirdo said.

I looked at Greg incredulously. I started the car and drove it back out onto the road, still struggling to process what Weirdo had just told us.

"Holy shit, dude… were you just finishing up at least?" I asked.

"No, actually they were on me pretty much as soon as I got out there."

"Dude, we were waiting on you for like fifteen minutes. What were you doing the whole time?" Greg said.

"Well, I just got started, so I just held eye contact with them while I pooped," Weirdo said.

I smelled something stinky. "Did you shit on yourself?" I asked.

"Oh, no, what you're probably smelling is the sock." He held up his sock. I could see it in the rearview mirror. I rolled down the back window.

"Throw it the fuck out! What did I tell you last time, you dingus?" I said.

"Sorry… I didn't want to litter right in front of those guys… that might've crossed a line," Weirdo said.

"But you were fine with holding eye contact with them for fifteen minutes while you shit, then removing your shoe, and proceeding to take off your sock and wipe your ass with it?" Greg said. Laughing was not exactly what we were doing. Howling uncontrollably was more like it.

"Oh yeah, they got a little edgy when I reached for my shoe, so I just did it real nice and slow. I wiped for a good while. Just didn't feel right leaving a dirty poopy sock right there, so I just held it afterward and backed off nice and slow."

"And you felt littering was crossing a line?" I asked.

"Yeah, and I'm also down a complete pair of socks now," Weirdo said.

Greg looked back. "That's fucking disgusting."

"I'm shocked that they didn't just shoot you," I said. "I kind of wish they had…" I clarified slightly under my breath.

"Well, they clearly could see that I needed a wipe, and I assumed they didn't have any."

"Why would you assume that?" Greg asked.

"I figure they would've offered," Weirdo responded.

"Jesus Christ," I muttered. Then I started chuckling uncontrollably, and just repeatedly broke into laughter whenever I even made a little eye contact with Greg or Weirdo. As we closed in on base, Weirdo became gaseous again, and I could see that he needed to shit… again. I decided that I wasn't gonna pull over. I rolled into the base with the windows down, cackling, eventually making it back to our barracks room with a great story to tell.

HIROSHIMA AIN'T GOT NOTHING ON ME

This story occurred when I just arrived to my unit after Airborne School.

John and I were two joes fresh out of school. We'd arrived to the ol' Eighty Deuce, and before us was our first weekend of freedom. We agreed on one thing: *must find girls*. We looked up the nearest college town, Raleigh. We booked a motel then went to the post exchange, where I grabbed a slick pink polo, some pink and blue shades, and orange and navy Oxfords.

"You see, John, in the club, you want to wear something attention grabbing," I said.

"Man, you look like a gay peacock," he said.

"You need to catch the ladies' attention. You know familiarity is a key part of attraction. By wearing these ostentatious clothes, my target will be forced to notice me at least a few times, which puts me at a competitive advantage over the sea of strangers I'll be competing against. So yeah… make fun of it all you want."

"Sure it will. I really regret agreeing to go out with you," John said.

"What're you wearing, man?" I said.

"Probably something less fruity." He did, wearing a basic button down, totally mid.

♦

We got to driving and we went to the motel. Since we were basically poor, we didn't want to pay for two rooms that neither of us would sleep in, so we split the cost for one room, in case one of us was unsuccessful. We agreed to try to go to the chicks' places. However, if necessary, a bro could use the room on a first-come, first-served basis. The other would just have to figure something else out. With this settled, we Axe body sprayed up and called an Uber.

"Hey, man, I'm feeling a bit nervous. Haven't talked to a girl in a while," John said.

"Well, don't be, they'll be just as drunk and stupid as we're about to be," I said.

"Nah man. You know we're in North Carolina, and I'm black. I don't know how I'm gonna be received," John said.

"What do you mean, hopefully with spread legs," I said. "Besides, this ain't the South of the fifties. Relax, man."

"Nah, I'm serious, man," John said. He did look genuinely a bit distraught.

"You'll be fine, just give 'em the terminator bit," I said, referencing the fact he was named after the main character from the Terminator, the savior of humanity.

"Some drunk college girl isn't going to understand a Terminator reference," John said.

"Well then, if she don't get it, move on until you find one that does. Simple," I said.

The Uber arrived and we got in.

♦

Since it was early, we made a detour to Dave N' Busters. I won prizes, ate funnel fries, cheese sticks, and nachos. I figured that I needed the carbs for all the banging I was gonna do. Around eleven p.m., I decided it was time. John was already tipsy and feeling a bit more confident. So we went.

♦

Club number one.

It's a small place, on the back side of the main strip. I spot some girls. I go to girls. I begin friendly conversation with girls and get girl's number. I then spot another group of girls. Same group of girls that John Connor is ogling. I look at him, he looks at me. We nod heads. We go. I see a hot girl on the left. I go to hot girl. Connor was going for the same girl. But I beat him. This flustered him, so he goes to the girl on the far edge.

I talk, get a number, then leave. This throws John off, who also leaves, sans number. We get a couple of drinks. I wave to the hot girl, giving her the "call me" sign.

We go to the next bar. It's a rowdy club and we have to wait in line. During this time, John is sobering up. He is beginning to lose confidence.

We get in, I get him a drink from the outer bar, and we walk inside.

Dead ahead of us, standing towards the entrance, I see three girls. I go right for the blonde. I talk her up. We exchange numbers. I try to leave. She hands me her drink, then runs off to the bathroom. She is too trusting, a good omen for me.

I stand there waiting for her to come back, like an idiot. John comes up to me. "Yo, that was pretty smooth, man. Think I need you to find out for me if one of her friend's names is Sarah."

"Haha, I will let you know. We can divide, liquor 'em up, and conquer," I said, tasting the blonde girl's drink, a lemon drop or some shit. She was obviously an amateur.

"Alright, Joe, first I'm gonna need another drink," John said.

I saw the girls approaching. "Yeah, you go get 'em, tiger!" I said. John disappeared into the gyrating mass and disorienting strobe lights.

I chatted with the blonde gal for a bit, you know, screaming into each other's ears. "You're smart!" said the girl into my ear. It was not a compliment I was expecting, and a bit random. Not sure why that was the thing she decided upon. I wondered if this was her equivalent of "you have a nice smile." Maybe smart was the new sexy. I began to lose confidence. I lost even more when John Connor finally reemerged. He grabbed me by the shoulder.

"Well... Well... Well... what do we have here?" John said. I turned towards him. Dear God, he looked worse than he sounded, with his eyebrows up and a rictus grin. You know the look—the "I'm seeing double, I'm so fucking smashed" one? Yeah, he was grinning like a cracked out homeless man, leaning against me for support, sloshing his drink.

"So which one of you is named... Sarah?" he said, pointing at them and spilling his drink. It appeared none of them were named Sarah. I knew that if this girl thought I was smart, a Terminator reference would just whir right over her and her friends' heads.

"Haha, ladies," I interrupted. "I think this man wants to buy one of you a drink?" I was hoping that one of them would take him up on it. "Yah, okay," they said in unison, like the Stepford wives. It caught me by surprise.

The blondie's two friends clomped off with my belligerently drunk friend. Me and blondie then made our way to the dance floor and proceeded to grind, grope, and make out. I was beginning to think things were looking up for me again. I got her outside, where we got a drink and made out some more. "You want to get out of here? I've got a room not too far from here," I said.

"I do. Just can't with the roommates, can't have them see. I'll text you later." We kissed, and I left and went to another bar, totally losing John. It was now 1:45. The clubs were shutting down. It was cold, and I was hungry.

Down the strip was this little taco and burrito bar. I texted John my location, and he said that he was en route. So he wasn't dead, which was good. And I was hungry, which was not. I got in line and ordered a XL burrito with nacho cheese sauce and sour cream. Since tonight was a bust—I doubted blondie would call—I decided that it didn't really matter. So I pounded that burrito. It was the most delicious burrito I've ever had. Nothing beats drunk food.

Connor linked up with me, and it seemed he was a bit soberer, but not too much more. He strolled in around two a.m. He too got a burrito and we ate in silence.

2:30 a.m. came. We'd called an Uber to get back to the motel.

My phone buzzed. "You up?" texted blondie from the bar.

"Sure am. Should I head over?" I texted.

"You should. Here's my address: 1456 Cum Dumpster Lane. And call me when you're here! I will need to sneak you in past my roommates!"

"Alright, I will see you then," I texted.

"Hey, John"—his head was teetering back and forth and might've wound up in his burrito—"I got booty called, so I'm gonna take off!" I said.

"Have fun, you faggy flamingo," John said.

With that, I turned and went to get my Uber. On the way over, I noticed a bit of rumbling in my stomach and suddenly felt a bit nervous.

I got to her place and called her up. Waited for her to come get me, my stomach gurgled. I probably had to fart. I realized I should probably try to squeak one out before she got down to me, and that's what I did—I squeaked one out. Then I heard a door open and there she was. Luckily it was quite breezy. We kissed real quick. Her intentions were obvious. It was on.

She slowly cracked open the door to her apartment. She dipped her head in, and looked around, then waved me in, gesturing for me to be quiet. We tiptoed our way across the common area and to her room. Once inside the room. I pushed her against the nearest wall, quietly, as you're supposed to do, and made out with her. But then I began to feel contractions in my lower colon: the funnel fries, mozzarella sticks, poppers, burritos, nachos, and beer did not care that I was about to get laid. I had to go. It wasn't just like: Oh, I could poop. Nor was it: Man, I better poop soon. It was more like: If I don't poop, I'm literally going to die.

So we're making out. I say as smoothly as I can, "I need to freshen up in the bathroom. Why don't you get ready for me?" She seemed to like it. I hoped she didn't hear how tense I was from holding back the levies. While she moved to the bed and turned on the television—all positive signs—I moved to the bathroom, quickly, but not too quickly.

Once inside, I lost all composure. I flipped every switch, hoping one of them was a fan. I dropped trousers, pit crew-fast, which nearly wasn't fast enough. Before my cheeks were kissed by cool porcelain, the shit was gushing out. First it came out like an avalanche, slushy-like with some boulders.

Then the torrent stopped suddenly. I felt a blockage in my butt. Something solid was following the chunkarrhea. My stomach knotted with pain as I pushed (but not too loudly) and braced myself against the shower door. As I looked down, I noticed a cute fluffy pink rug.

Long story short, I took one hell of a shit, definitely one of my top five biggest ever. It was one of those special occasion poops where the stars line up just right. I'd had the perfect storm of a week straight of new DFAC food, Tex-Mex, sour cream, and beer. It was destiny.

I got the last of the poop out. I listened carefully and just heard the TV. It seemed that I was good to proceed with banging this chick. I wiped up, then flushed.

This is where things went wrong.

Evidently, NC State dorms were still a bit antiquated; they suffered from old narrow pipes and relied on high-volume gravity flush toilets. Consequently, when I flushed, the thing clogged, and gallons of water poured into the bowl. The water continued to rise. Seeing what was about to happen, I scrambled around for a plunger. There was none to be found.

It seems that blondie had never properly challenged the toilet.

Then it happened. It began to slosh and spill over the side, and shit water spilled onto the pink fluffy rug. The smell was something fierce. I turned on the faucet so that she couldn't hear me battling her plumbing. I contemplated my next move.

This was definitely a mood killer. If blondie saw what I did in here, I would almost certainly not get laid. I must prevent her from using the bathroom at all costs. I pulled my britches up, made sure I hadn't stepped in anything, and locked the door from the inside behind me. I went to the bed feeling quite guilty.

But I banged her anyway and did not mention what I had done.

◆

Next day I woke up in her bed. I sensed her stirring, like she was about to get up. I did not want her to even approach her bathroom and risk her smelling it. So we fucked again.

She walked me out. I promised I'd call her.

I called an Uber from the street. It was ten minutes away. Too far away. As soon as she was out of sight, I began to move, trying to get as far away from her form as possible. I knew that she wouldn't be able to get into her bathroom, but would smell something terrible and eventually discover what I had done. I probably wouldn't get a chance to hook up with her again.

I wondered how she would explain the toilet situation, because she would run into a bit of a conundrum. Either she could preserve her perceived innocence by taking ownership of the giant shit, or she could admit to banging the guy who did. Sometimes, I wonder what choice she made.

I went ahead and blocked her number; I didn't know if this was something I could get sued for, but I wasn't about to take any risks.

I got in my Uber, with some Indian guy who wanted to hear about my "Walk of Shame."

"Well, I blew a girl's back out, and her toilet." I told him what had happened. We laughed, but I sensed that he thought less of me.

I got back to my motel and found Connor sleeping face down with his shoes still on.

Moral: You don't have to be a genius to be a boss, just an asshole.

RLTW

This story occurred when I attended Ranger Assessment and Selection Program (RASP). Army Rangers are one of the U.S. military's elite special operations groups. They are America's premier raid force—the guys you call when you want a lot of stuff dead but don't want to use a bomb.

It was my second year in the Army, and I was looking for something "hooah." I talked to the Ranger recruiter, and not too long afterward found myself in the middle of RASP. I was excited—albeit nervous—when I first showed up and reported to Pre-RASP. A couple of friends I'd made during Advanced Individual Training (AIT), both fit and driven individuals, reported in with me. They impressed me, and I was excited to be surrounded by likeminded individuals who refused to settle for mediocrity and strove for excellence.

During our first night there, I was setting up my bunk, making sure that the corners were tucked and folded, just as every other bed along the row of mattresses were—making sure everything was dress right dress. Suddenly, there was a commotion toward the back of the room where the latrines were.

"Everyone, get back here. It's happening!" All the beds emptied, and everyone scrambled toward the latrine. I looked at my buddies, who shrugged their shoulders. We decided to go see for ourselves what all the ruckus was about.

Inside the bathroom, the guys thronged around a single bathroom stall. Many stood on their tippy toes trying to peek over the top to see what was happening inside. People were chanting, "Do it! Do it!" I chimed in because I wanted to be included. Eventually I made my way toward the front and got a front-row seat to the event.

Inside the stall, one man squatted. Pants down, dick out, sweat beading down his bright red face. Behind him another guy had a hand outstretched over the toilet and beneath the other man's ass. His face was turning green, and he looked like he was about to vomit. To my horror—and to the pleasure and cheers of everyone else—the squatter pushed and released a torrent of explosive diarrhea which covered the other guy's hand and hit the edge of the toilet seat. The splatter was audible, and the stench was horrifying.

The gentleman, who I assume had lost a bet, had gotten more than he bargained for. Obviously, he knew that he was getting his hand pooped on, but I don't think he anticipated the runniness or velocity of the poop. Not only was his hand covered in feces, but it was running down his forearm, and some of the poop and toilet water had splattered onto his shirt and face. This unfortunate moron jerked his hand back, looked at it, then proceeded to projectile vomit all over the shit-covered toilet.

The would-be Rangers screamed and yelled approvingly, except for a few unlucky spectators who were also within splash range of the event. They jumped down off the stall's walls and proceeded to vomit into the nearby urinals. The man with poop on his hand began to panic. "Someone get me soap!"

"We're out of soap, the cadre haven't restocked it yet," someone said over the howling cackles that resonated off the walls of the latrine. Someone produced a bottle of bleach, which they proceeded to dump copiously over his shit-covered arm. The man who had provided the feces proceeded to wipe his ass in front of everyone—while laughing, I would add. There was no way, I thought, these guys would ever become Rangers.

As it turned out, I was wrong—very wrong. Both of them went on to have illustrious careers within the regiment.

"Guys! *Guys!* The cadre are heading up here!" someone yelled.

"Oh shit," I replied.

"Guys, we need to clean this up before he sees it!" someone else shouted.

And so began our mad dash to clean up the vomit and shit that these two Ranger candidates had so dutifully spread across the linoleum. All we had to clean it up was toilet paper and bleach.

Somehow, we got it cleaned up, and mercifully, the cadre did not enter the bathroom on that particular occasion.

(One week later)

I was still in Pre-RASP, sitting on the hot rocks, waiting for our usual smoke session from the sadistic cadre. It was toward the end of the day, and one of the cadre had brought his dog with him to work. We were hoping for an early release and perhaps a bit of a break from the constant onslaught of what we considered punishment.

Our class leader bellowed, "Everyone form up!" I hurriedly gathered my rucksack and threw it on. I made sure that my uniform was looking spiffy and went over the Ranger Creed in my mind, in case I was called upon to recite it. If a random person was called and messed up the creed, that meant everyone was going to get punished.

We formed up along the sidewalk, making sure everyone was "dress right dress" and standing in neat little rows. With the time we had, we checked each other's uniforms, making sure that there wasn't any fraying and that our flags were crisp and horizontal.

The cadre came out, his big German Shepherd strolling alongside him on the rocks in front of us. He walked up and down the ranks inspecting us, giving us a look over, while his giant dog took a spiteful shit on the rocks where we had to sit. Luckily, he found no flaw within our ranks; we passed his inspection.

"Stand by for further instruction," he told our student leader. The cadre walked back into the building with his dog in tow, leaving us standing rigidly in formation. We didn't dare move, lest he was still watching us, waiting for us to crack. Unfortunately, we did.

"Hey Dolton, I dare you to pick up that dog's poo!"

I stood still and muttered, "No, no, no," under my breath, but the majority were about it. Dolton broke rank, waltzed out to the middle of the rock pit and reached down, and with his bare hand, he grasped the steaming pile of dog shit. He then held it up above him like a Mayan holding up the beating heart of his enemy.

"Front leaning rest position! Move!" The cadre's voice bellowed from inside the building.

"Damn it," I muttered as I got down into the push-up position and proceeded to get smoked because the future Ranger sergeant major decided to break rank and pick up a dog turd.

(A few weeks later)

Sometime later, I found myself in the middle of the Ranger Assessment and Selection Program, out enjoying the pleasures of Cole Range (a.k.a. Ranger Hell Week), which is infamous for being a four-day sleep- and food-deprived smoke fest. You carry sandbags around all day, sprint two hundred yards back and forth, again and again, to the fabled wood line, and, among other things, are woken up in the middle of the night for forced ruck marches. My feet were covered in blisters, I'd bled through my boots, I was delirious, and here I was out enjoying the most relaxing part of the whole endeavor—land navigation at night.

I only bring this up to recollect yet another encounter of the fecal variety. I'd found a point and laid down at a nearby tree to begin planning my route to the next point when I felt something wet and sticky that was intensely fragrant. I realized then and there that I'd laid in someone's shit. Now throughout the rest of my time at Cole Range, I smelled like poop. And not just anyone's poop—my bunkmate's poop. Later, he proudly informed me that he'd dropped "a fat turd" next to this point by a ravine. After some discourse, we realized that we'd had the same point, and I'd laid in the exact spot where he'd decided to drop a landmine.

This was awesome because I had to keep my clothes and pack them in my bag. And after repeated smoke sessions, and "bag dumps" that the cadre made us do periodically, the shit really got mixed in with the rest of my things quite nicely. For the rest of my time in RASP and Pre-RASP again, I would enjoy the noxious odors of his MRE-fueled poop.

(Seven weeks later)

Yup, I failed RASP, twice. Failed push-ups four times. It was a big kick in the nuts. I had gone in confident, but I came out a two-time Cole Range survivor with nothing to show for it. I found myself in what is possibly the most depressing company in all the Army, known colloquially as "World-Wide."

World-Wide is the company that you go to when you've either quit, failed, or got kicked out of RASP. It is not a place you want to be—it is the end of the road and the end of the dream for many. It was not what I had planned. In World-Wide, you don't get smoked quite as bad, but they compensate by treating you like absolute garbage. The cadre mock and parade you in front of the guys who are still in the suck of RASP; it is a deeply shameful feeling.

Things were particularly interesting though as the noncommissioned officer (NCO) in charge of World-Wide was something of a legend. Adding to his legend was his unusual way of conducting himself. He drove around in a souped-up pony car, was middle-aged, divorced, and had a detachment peculiar to someone who has taken many lives. He spoke in staccato and was always serious. He would chastise us for the littlest things and looked upon all of us failures with disgust.

It was nine p.m., they had cut the lights off, and we were all going to sleep in our bunks. Then the lights flicked on.

"Everyone get the fuck out your beds."

My heart skipped a beat, and I went into motion, finding my shoes and getting to the position of attention. After nearly twenty weeks of RASP and pre-RASP, I was accustomed to being roused from sleep to get smoked. I stood there waiting for a punishment alongside the other members of World-Wide. At the front of the room plodded in the crusty NCO. He lumbered in front of us, his head bobbing and swiftly turning like an emu's as he eyed us one by one. My nuts began to up-suck in anticipation of the smoke session.

"Men..." he began, "Are we animals? Or are we just like the no-good uncivilized hadjis? I didn't fight no war to come home to this obscene depravity."

I racked my brain to figure out what had happened. I thought maybe he caught someone with contraband or whacking off.

"Never in my life have I ever felt so disgusted as I do right now with you sad, pathetic sacks of shit," he continued. "Men, I want to know who did it." He paused in the room and slowly swept his eyes across everyone.

"Who had the *audacity* to drop a big, fat shit in my barrack's toilet and not flush it?" he hissed. I thought he was joking. If I weren't sure I was about to get wrecked, I would've laughed, but at the time this seemed like an altogether serious matter and a grave offense.

"Men... the poop in question is large—so large that it is poking out of the water and onto the front edge of the bowl and releasing a putrid stench into the air. Which one of you did it?" he inquired. He walked up in front of me and demanded, "Was it you?" His eyes flickered up and down as if he was trying to imagine the giant shit coming out of my ass. "How about you?" he said as he moved onto the next guy, much to my relief. He went down the line like this continuing his inspection. "What is particularly strange about this very large, disgusting, brutish shit is that there was no toilet paper. Men, even Al-Qaeda has the decency to clean themselves up afterward. But one of you lowlifes did something despicable, left it there for everyone else to see, and didn't even bother to clean themselves up afterward. Men, this night can go one of two ways.

"First, the perp can come forward and come clean, and apologize to me and everyone else, or we can stay up all night," he said. Silence ensued, and no one budged.

"Very well. Men, take a lap and meet me by the rock pit," he said. We began beating feet to the stairs and outside the building. As we ran around the building, the whining began: "Who took the poop? Who did it? Come forward, you pussy!" someone said.

I started laughing.

"What's so fucking funny, Joe?" the whiner said.

"You know, I think we should all poop in the same toilet without flushing, out of solidarity," I said.

"Shut the fuck up. I bet you did it!" someone said.

I, in fact, wasn't the culprit, although no one came forward.

(Several hours later)

We returned to our barracks and were instructed to go to sleep. The lights flicked off, and we waited. We heard his pony car roar to life and peel off. Me and a couple of guys jumped down from our bunks.

"What the fuck are you doing? Get back in bed!" the whiner said. We shushed him and made our way to the bathroom. It was in stall three that we found the source of our vexation. An impressively long and girthy deuce lay pristinely across the bowl. Indeed, it did peak out of the water. We admired it for a while before flushing it down, which took a couple of tries. We returned to our bunks, not giving a fuck, thinking this was all some sort of joke.

I always had a feeling it was a cadre member who had done this. I believe that we'd been framed. We were limited to three measly meals a day. None of us in World-Wide were consuming enough protein to have produced such a large dense turd. Someone had it out for us.

I guess if there's a moral to this story it's to never shit on yourself, because the world will shit on you. And when you're shit out of luck, remember it could always be shittier!

THRILLA IN MANILA

This story occurred shortly after arriving at my Special Forces ODA. For those of you reading this book who were/are not military, ODAs are Operational Detachment Alphas, highly trained, like all the other Special Forces.

My teammate and I had been boozing at a local bar after a day of training Philippine Special Forces units on comms and shooting skills. It had been a long tedious day of screaming at the locals and trying to overcome thick accents and language barriers. It was exhausting work, something that felt beneath soldiers of our caliber. But at least our commander had given us the okay to cruise the streets and hit the bars.

It was another humid night in Manila. I strolled the street with a teammate. Like any red-blooded American Special Forces, we were looking for chicks. Our teams and teams before us had an illustrious history of getting laid and starting secret second families, and we'd be remiss if we didn't uphold the time-honored tradition of banging as many locals as we possibly could. Our team's honor depended on it.

Since I was the newest team member, the pressure was on me to get laid. After all, if I couldn't infiltrate a girl's panties, how could I be expected to infiltrate a jihadist compound? Or so was the logic offered to me by the team's weapons sergeant. I disagreed, but I was looking for a win tonight, in order to have a story to share in the team room come Monday morning. I needed to earn their respect. For the past two weeks every other guy had come in with some epic story of debauchery and "fucking the shit out of some girl." I would not turn up empty-handed.

The bar scene was good. There were all sorts of girls crawling about, and also things that seemed female but upon closer inspection were not. I was not having the best luck with the females at the bar, and was becoming drunker and worried that I might wind up going back home with a tranny, which would make me this week's laughing stock. I was tired of getting swindled. I decided to deviate from the plan. My teammate was up at the bar with some girl in his lap who was asking him for drinks.

"Hey Rick, I'm gonna go down the street to another bar."

"Cool, man!" he said as he paid for another drink for the lady he was with. I exited the bar, went out into the humid Manila air, and called a taxi.

My teammates had told me about this one strip downtown, near some of the grungier bars. They said that I would be able to find some prostitutes walking the curb and would have my pick of the ladies. Being the esteemed scholar and special operator that I was, I decided to take the deep dive. The taxi pulled up to a dimly lit curb, and I stepped out and asked the driver to wait for me, offering him a ten-dollar bill. The group of girls along the curb smoking cigarettes straightened themselves out as I approached.

An older woman, who I assumed to be the madame, approached me.

"How you do today, sir?" the madame said.

"Good, I need a hot chick," I said.

"Ow, yes, we got a lot of byutiful leydies here tunayt," the madame said. She snapped her fingers and the ladies lined up in front of me along the sidewalk.

"You may chus wan." She held up a single digit for emphasis in front of a crooked smile. I studied the ladies, looking them up and down. They weren't exactly tens; each of them had their flaws: too fat, too old, too ugly, too much penis, etc. I studied them up and down, wishing that I could mix and mash their bits and amalgamate one hot girl. Like take the second girl's boobs, the fifth girl's figure, and the third girl's ass.

After some contemplation, I decided on a twenty-something-year-old lady who seemed cute enough but was firmly in the "too much makeup" category. To elaborate, she looked like her makeup had been done by Joaquin Phoenix, a bit clownish, some might say. I figured I could probably get her to wash off the makeup; she was salvageable, unlike too old and too much penis. I gave the madame twenty bucks, and the hooker in clown makeup and I got into the back of the taxi.

I instructed the taxi to take me to a nearby hotel. I decided against taking her back to my place. I didn't want her to be able to easily find me in the event she became pregnant or was part of some kind of spy organization. Then again, I doubt a spy would've put on what amounted to clown makeup.

"So, uh, what's your name?" I asked the hooker.

"My name... is... Lyyyrra," she said, struggling with her English.

Quickly I could tell that there was a serious language barrier, which felt a bit too insurmountable to me. I decided to remain silent for the duration of our drive to the hotel. After all, I wasn't paying her for conversation.

We arrived at the hotel, I paid the driver, and we walked into what was obviously the local "here's where you take your hooker" hotel. It was immediately apparent to anyone who saw us what was going on. I looked every bit the sex tourist, a big American guy with a Philippine chick in clown makeup wearing stilettos, booty shorts, and a crop top. My activities were glaringly obvious. But luckily the nice receptionist spoke English and promptly gave us a room.

We moved on down the hallway, took the elevator up, and arrived at the room. It was my first time with a hooker so I wasn't exactly sure how things were supposed to proceed, but I knew what the end state should be. She put down her purse and began shimming out of her booty shorts and top. I stopped her.

"Hey, you know… I don't like your makeup. Would you mind taking a shower and getting it off?" I asked. The hooker looked rather perplexed.

"You wan tu… make out dadi?" she said.

"No—" I shook my head. "I… I just need you to wash your face," I said, trying to enunciate the words as best as I could. Her eyes widened.

"You no like face?" she asked me, pointing to her face.

"Yes, me no like face," I responded, nodding my head. I then showed her to the bathroom, turned on the shower, and gestured for her to go in. She undressed and awkwardly stepped into the shower; she looked sideways at me smiling nervously.

"Ow yu wan tu watch me?" the hooker said.

"No," I said, then I pointed to the water. "You," I pointed at her. "Wash," I made a scrubbing motion of my face. "Face," I pointed to her face.

She smiled sheepishly at me. The language was proving a greater barrier than I anticipated, and I think she might've thought this was some weird sex thing. Or perhaps she was worried that I was going to cut her organs out and sell them on the black market. In hindsight, that could've funded the acquisition of a shitload more hookers. Clearly, she was still not getting it.

I pointed at the soap, and then pointed at her face. I pointed to my face and made a scrubbing motion again. At last, she seemed to understand and began using soap and water to remove the ghoulish makeup; all of those times playing charades had finally paid off. Satisfied, I stepped outside of the bathroom, and waited for her to finish up. I glanced at my watch and began removing my own clothes and mentally prepared myself to bang a hooker.

She was taking a while. Longer than necessary, it seemed. I had her for an hour and I planned on getting the most bang for my buck. She was taking longer than I would've liked, and I

Department of Degenerates • 39

considered flushing the toilet to expedite her shower. Eventually she emerged from the bathroom, naked, slick, svelte, without makeup.

She would do.

She started strong. She came up, kneeled down beside the bed, and gave me head. Already I was beginning to feel better about all of this.

Soon thereafter, we transitioned. I got on top of her and she guided me inside her. She made stereotypical Asian moaning sex sounds, and it was working for me. I began railing her with aplomb and gusto.

I was nearing climax when a noxious odor hit me. I couldn't figure out what it was. It smelled like raw sewage but I kept pounding away, trying to reach my end state. But the odor not only lingered but worsened. Maybe she just slipped a fart.

The smell was ruining it for me, so I moved us to the other side of the bed and flipped her around for some doggy. Shit was running out of her ass crack, down the back of her pussy, and dribbling down towards my cock.

This hooker had literally shit herself, while fucking me.

I had literally fucked the shit out of her.

I was both appalled, but also slightly impressed with myself. The worse part, though, was that she didn't even seem to notice.

"Mmmmm, yu fuck me real gud, daddy," she said. I shook my head. I asked her to get up and guided her back into the shower, trying to bring the shit to her attention. This time I pointed at her ass and made vigorous scrubbing motions, then pointed at the soap.

"Poop," I said. "Your ass." I pointed towards her ass.

Eventually she got the message. She was getting much better at charades. She smiled sheepishly then began washing her ass vigorously.

While she showered, I surveyed the bed and discovered a shit stain where she had been laying. It smelled pretty bad. Luckily there was some Febreze on the nightstand, which I sprayed liberally until the room smelled like a tropical porta-potty. Oddly enough, though, I was still pretty horny, and realized that I still had about thirty minutes left with this hooker, on whom I'd spent a good twenty dollars of my own hard-earned cash.

As a Special Forces soldier, I took pride in my ability to problem-solve and overcome any obstacles. So I went into the bathroom, grabbed a towel, and threw it down on the bed. When the hooker was done rinsing the poop off, I laid her back down on the towel, ass down, and resumed banging her. I fucked her even more furiously than before this time, and to her credit, she was unflappable, and performed great Asian moaning and all. But she continued to shit herself.

Though she shit the bed again, and the room smelled fucking awful, I wasn't upset. I was delighted with the experience. Not only had I overcome language barriers and a spastic colon, but I'd also walked away with what I was sure was going to be the best story in the team room come Monday morning.

You see, they may say that they "fucked the shit out of some girl" but I'm the only one that can say he actually has.

PART 2

BARRACKS BUNNIES AND STRIPPERS

THE SCIENCE OF BARRACKS BUNNIES

This is an educational aside.

Your traditional barracks bunny usually gets a guest access card because they are dating or were previously dating someone who lived in the barracks. Though a barracks bunny's relationship status has no bearing whatsoever on her actions, they come to the parties alone and with salacious intent. Barracks bunnies come in all sorts of shapes and sizes—none of them hot. When not getting ramped out by lower enlisted, barracks bunnies can be found flunking their community college classes or working the day shift at a Burger King.

Barracks scientists have long researched the barracks bunny phenomenon and have developed a general theory of barracks bunnies. Barracks bunnies, through a series of unfortunate events, wind up in a military town, where the ratio of males to females is in their favor. Moreover, they are surrounded by fit and sexually frustrated military men, many of whom do not have cars and are unable to expand their search for women beyond the immediate area. Strategically, the barracks bunny is very well positioned. Once the barracks bunny has figured this out and developed the taste for enlisted men, she will begin scavenging for men more aggressively. At some point, through Tinder, she will wind up making a match with Private McDreamy.

Private McDreamy takes the soon-to-be barracks bunny into his barracks room and ramps her out. It is here, in the hallways of a multi-storied barracks filled with thousands of enlisted men, that she has her eureka moment. She notices the stares and the multitude of men in uniform checking her out. She realizes that in the barracks, she is the only girl and therefore the most desirable. She has her pick of thousands of fit, hypercompetitive, and often drunk men who all want to bang her; she is happy to oblige. The barracks bunny gets Private Mcdreamy to sponsor her for a guest pass. She begins inquiring about the barracks life and learns when the parties are. The barracks bunny returns to the barracks on a Friday night, attends a party, ditches Private McDreamy, and proceeds to disappear with one guy after another, returning to the party without them to pick off another soldier.

As the night progresses and the barracks becomes more intoxicated, she becomes bolder. She begins knocking on doors like a Jehovah's Witness, offering up her pussy straight away. She eventually will pass out in some soldier's room, deep into her conquest. She awakes sore and goes on a scavenger hunt throughout the barracks trying to find different clothing items. Eventually she leaves the barracks emerging like a butterfly from a cocoon, fully metamorphized into the barracks bunny. Hooked, she would return again and again, ravaging entire wings with STIs.

BLUE BALLS AND GREEN WEENIES

After having my bursa burst and being put on a six-week profile, I said goodbye to my friends, and felt alone for the first time in a while—that is, until I met another unfortunate soul named Jake. As people came and went, Jake and I found camaraderie.

Finding a friend didn't exactly improve our morale. Instead, we amplified one another's vehemence. Every day we'd wake up with even lousier attitudes than the day before and go about our day half-assing details. This is where we both cut our teeth as shammers. Everyone in the Army becomes salty at one point or another, because inevitably, everyone gets dicked down by the Green Weenie.

"Green Weenie" is a term often used in the United States military, particularly in the Army and Marine Corps, to refer to a mystical and malevolent force that signifies the inexplicable, incompetent, or arbitrary actions and decisions made by various military echelons that make life suck. Examples of this include: "mandatory fun," weekend recall formations, being denied leave, missing children's birthdays, CQ duty, chute shake detail, getting assigned to Fort Polk, etc. Many enlisted soldiers I've talked to, especially older NCOs, get a haunted look in their eye when you bring up ol' Green Weenie. They speak about it in hushed tones to other enlisted men, cursing their superiors for their incipient ideas and themselves for joining the service.

Now Jake and I were getting real fed up with everything. Our freedoms had been further restricted after some new kid got caught trying to go off post with a girl. We were having formations every hour on the hour from 0630 to 1900. Technically, we were not allowed to leave the barracks. Understandably, the cadre were apprehensive about giving a bunch of basic training graduates too much leeway lest they get into trouble and have their stay extended at what was supposed to be a transitory unit. But this was proving anything but transitory. Already they had extended my profile after the first round of antibiotics had failed.

We were getting fed up with being treated like cattle and not being allowed to go anywhere. Already we'd figured out that after the final formation on Friday the cadre wouldn't show up again until breakfast time the next day. We had a pretty good idea of who would be in charge of us and when; we had their patterns figured out, thanks to our long stay there.

We were cleaning up the battalion building, closing it out before the weekend. While mopping a floor, we'd found a list in a display case near the battalion entrance.

"Yo, Joe, check this out," Jake said. I quit pretending to mop and ambled over to the document in the display case on the wall. It was a list of locations along with addresses, including arcades, shooting ranges, sporting goods stores, and strip clubs.

"Man, they literally just blacklisted anything that could even be remotely considered fun," I said.

"Haha, yup... damn, there are a fuck load of strip clubs in the area," Jake said.

"There sure fucking are," I said.

"You know, after final formation, we won't see any cadre until tomorrow," Jake said.

"True, I suppose we might take advantage of that," I said.

We decided to sneak out after the final formation. We settled on a place and planned our escape. We ordered a taxi, surreptitiously moved into the parking lot behind battalion, and then headed towards one of the blacklisted strip clubs.

We arrived at a lone, dark, windowless building that was definitely on the wrong side of town. The place looked like it was closed. Undeterred, we made our way around the backside of the building where a dark overhang and a single "guard" stood outside. He was Black and wore a fur coat. I was getting hardcore pimp vibes. Before we said anything, he waved us in. We walked past him and into the dark entrance of the building.

Inside, the place was dimly lit by neon lights. The front receptionist didn't even check our IDs, instead demanding that we pay a cover charge of twenty dollars each. We gladly paid and then made our way back toward the lounge. We hadn't made it ten feet when two obese Black women in lingerie accosted us. One of them grabbed me by the collar and dragged me to a foldout chair. The stripper pushed me down into the chair, then proceeded to straddle me. Her considerable heft cut off circulation to my legs, and unfortunately, she was already breathing heavily, right into my face, her breath smelled like Newports. To the side of us, a man wearing gold chains and a durag (clearly a bouncer?) pulled up a chair and watched as the girl (and I use the word loosely) "danced" on my lap.

Before I could even react, the lady (again, for lack of a more descriptive word) dismounted me and began shoving her ass in my face. Immediately, the smell of shit hit my face, and I noticed stretch marks on her ass. I feared she would give me pink eye.

"You know, I need to get a drink." I began to stand up to try and get away. But the stripper whipped around and put her hands on my both of my thighs, pinning me down. She pursed her lips and made what I suppose she thought to be a sexy face. She stared deeply into my eyes. I tried not to stare at the giant mole on her upper lip or her blonde wig. She then did something that haunts me to this day. She cocked back, made a gargling sound, and spat a foamy, mucusy snot rocket at my junk.

I was wearing jeans and nearly recoiled, but she held me firmly in place via her three-hundred-plus pounds of heft. She then placed her mouth onto the mucus wad on my crotch. And made a vacuum-sucking sound. She then lifted her head off of my crotch, a good foot or two. Between her mouth and my crotch, there was a tendril of drool connecting us. I bolted upward and began to walk away to try to retrieve my buddy. But the dude in a durag who'd been watching us stood up between me and the exit.

"I believe you owe this lady for the dance," he said.

I shook my head. "I didn't fucking ask for that!" I said. The guy lifted his shirt and I saw the shiny glint of metal.

"I believe you owe her a hundred dollas," he said. I looked at him, back at the fat troll who'd just spat on my crotch, and then back over at my buddy, Jake. He was in a similar position, except for the fact that he was throwing money in the air and seemed to be enjoying it. Begrudgingly, I gave them their hundred dollars and tried to get Jake's attention.

Jake continued to be defiled for two entire songs. While I waited for my buddy to finish up, I debated calling the cops, but I knew that if I did, my young Army career would likely be over and/or made much worse.

Finally, he came over to me. "Dude, Candy gave me her phone number and she said that if I'm free later I should hit her up." His enthusiasm caused me to do a double take. I confirmed Candy was indeed obese, and I marveled at the appropriateness of her name.

"Oh, goody, maybe you can smoke crack and help her with her insulin shots while you're at it," I said.

"Insulin shots?"

"She weighs more than both of us combined, dipshit. Come on, let's get out of here before we get shot or catch something that needs penicillin to get rid of."

We moved outside, and I saw that there weren't any Ubers nearby for another 30 minutes at least. A group of shady guys began congregating in the parking lot of the establishment we'd just left, and they were eyeballing us pretty hard. We decided to get the fuck out of there.

We walked down the street about a mile or two and tried hailing a taxi in the parking lot of a very seedy motel, but with no luck. That's when, across the street, I spotted a glowing neon sign: "XXX."

"Hey, man, want to go check out that store?" I asked, pointing across the street.

"Hell yeah," Jake said.

We darted across the road and towards the seedy porn store. It was much bigger on the inside than it appeared from the outside. It was a sex-store Mecca. To this day, nothing I've seen comes close. Everything from limp dragon-dick dildos and vibrating silicone feet to sex playgrounds and full size sex robots. It had an ample library of both DVDs and VHS cassettes. We were in awe of the impressive place, and barely noticed the two creepy old men loitering in a corner.

We perused the sex shop, as two straight dudes do. I grabbed a telescopic lightsaber dildo and was like, "Yo, look at this thing, you could beat someone to death with it."

"Yeah, the cops should make it a standard issue baton," Jake said.

"Think it comes in green?" I said.

"Probably," Jake said.

"You ever see a pink flamingo prank?" I said. Jake shook his head. "It's where you get those plastic flamingos and put like a hundred of them in someone's lawn."

"Man, is that what ya'll do in Kansas for fun?" Jake asked.

"Shut up. Anyways, I was thinking we could get a bunch of green ones and litter the cadre hut. You know, Green Weenie them back," I said.

"Yeah, that's a real shitty idea," Jake said. I concurred. Besides, they were far too expensive.

We went around the shop, exploring. Then I spotted a dark hallway in the back of the store, close to where the creepy old guys were standing. Naturally, we went toward the dark hallway, and there was a little ticket booth at the front. When we got there, one of the creepy old guys came out from behind the booth to assist us. He was hunched over, deeply wrinkled, and had a severe underbite, replete with long grey strands of stringy greasy hair sprouting from a balding head. He reminded me of Herbert the pervert from the Simpsons. I couldn't see his eyes due to the glow coming off his rectangular glasses.

"Would you gentleman like a ticket?" he asked.

"No, just looking," I said. Past him I saw lines of booths side by side. I wondered what they were. The cashier then handed me a coin. "Here's one on the house," he said, handing my buddy one too. Admittedly, I was pretty curious, so I took the coin and went down the dark hallway. I could feel that everyone was watching me, but I remained undeterred. I selected a booth, opened the door, and went inside.

Inside there was a plush red chair, next to it a box of Kleenex, and on the wall a touchscreen monitor. Quickly I deduced that this must be some kind of masturbation booth. I'd never heard of anything like this, and I was both intrigued and disgusted. The room was quite dark, and I was afraid to touch anything. On the screen ran ads for porn movies. I was, as I said, absolutely appalled. How can any sick fucking creepy animal come in here and jerk off in a public facility? The indignity of it.

But I hadn't busted a nut in months, so I sat down and began seeing what movies were on the thing.

That's when I heard a door shut, and felt my room shake a little. I heard footsteps and the chair in the room to my left groaned under someone's weight. *Why the fuck would Jake pick the room right next to mine?* I thought. Naturally I turned my head to the left and discovered a large hole in the wall. Through the hole I saw the silhouette of a balding man and the glint of his spectacles; it was the creepy cashier. His intent was obvious. I snapped upright, pulled my pants up, and got the hell out of there.

Thankfully Jake still hadn't selected a booth.

"*Dude*, we have got to go!" I said.

"Can't we call an Uber first?"

"Nope, we're gonna start walking, now." Behind me I heard the door to the masturbation room open and knew that creepy guy was behind us. I grabbed Jake by the shoulder and we speedily walked out of the store and down the sketchy hood. I explained what happened to Jake.

"No! That creepy old guy is still trying to get his groove on? Or should I say, he's still able to?" He was mind-blown. "I guess coming out here was a mistake," he said.

"Definitely, but good decisions never result in memorable nights," I said.

We got an Uber and managed to get back into our barracks rooms undetected. The next day I told everyone about getting gobbed on by an obese stripper, swindled by a pimp, and the jerk-off rooms with glory holes. Quickly my future classmates came to me, wanting me to regale them with my grand tale. I had friends. Totally worth it.

Some guys had a lot of follow-up questions and seemed to want to know the name of the place. I wonder if any of them went down there and encountered the creepy glory hole operator.

FAYETTENAM'S FINEST

It was a weekday. I was a Special Forces Candidate, and we hadn't seen any girls in a while.

"Wanna go to a strip club?" Greg asked.

"Sure, why not." I responded.

We got into my shitty car and drove off post towards a cluster of strip clubs. At the time of writing this, it probably wouldn't be a stretch to say that there are at least ten strip clubs along this little, sketchy stretch of road just outside of base. There were so many places that, to bring in customers on a Wednesday night, they were offering discounted dances, free drinks, buffets, and all the strip club swag.

"Where should we go first?" I asked.

"A buddy said that Venessa's has the hottest girls," Greg said.

"Sounds like a plan."

We pulled into the little parking lot at Venessa's and headed toward the entrance. It was a small, dingy-looking building on a strip with eclectic shops. It looked dilapidated, run down, and like it would be crawling with cockroaches. A true elysian getaway, at least by comparison to the offerings on base. We hopped out of the vehicle and headed through the rusty doors. We entered a narrow hallway that bypassed the check-in stand.

"Cover charge is twenty dollas," said an old washed-up stripper in a thick New Jersey accent.

"Twenty dollars?" I said.

"Yeah, twenty dollas per person," she said. I looked back at Greg, who had begun reaching for his wallet.

"Hang on, buddy, how do we even know this shit is worth it?" I tried walking past the counter to get a peek at what was happening deeper inside of the club, but an enormous bouncer stepped in front of me.

"You gotta pay to go in here," said the stripper. I muttered some profanities.

"How about we just go down the street and find another place?" I said.

Greg shook his head. "Twenty dollars probably means they're grade A, bro," he said. I could see some logic to this. Perhaps they could staff higher quality strippers here, as we believed them to have.

"Alright." I huddled up closer to him. "How about I just get a ticket, go in there and scope the place out, and if it's good, then you can get a ticket too. If not, we just take off."

"Yeah, sounds like a plan, bro."

I grabbed a ticket and went in without him. I walked down the long corridor and into a red felt lined room that had chairs and couches surrounding the stage. The place was empty, except for a lone stripper, who danced erratically on a pole. She was painfully white, emaciated, and had hair falling out and yellowed teeth. She locked eyes with me from across the room, since I was the only patron in the establishment, then hobbled at me like a zombie that hadn't come across fresh brains in months, her already awkward gait made worse by the six-inch heels she was wearing. Her yellowed smile snarled to one side, and her cock-eyed expression—which she perhaps thought was sexy—looked like the rictus pose of the walking dead.

Not looking to repeat the experience I'd had with the obese stripper, I fled. Back down the tunnel, grabbing Greg on my way.

"Bro! This place sucks. Let's get out of here… NOW!" We trotted back to my car, and I glanced over my shoulder to see if the creature had trailed me. It seemed she had not. Perhaps she'd snapped her femur whilst in pursuit.

I told Greg about what happened.

"Huh, no way bro. I've heard so many great things about the place. Maybe it was just like that because its three p.m. on Wednesday," Greg said. It occurred to me that he might be right.

"Where to next?" I said.

"How about we try Starlight Cabaret? I've heard good things about it."

Even seedier than Venessa's, this particular strip club was in another part of town on a lonely corner, nestled next to an abandoned gas station, behind a warehouse. It was a two-storied squalor that looked like it might've formerly been some kind of medical office. We walked in through the rotating doors to what looked to have been a former patient waiting room. There was a receptionist window and faded outlines on the linoleum of former kiosks, chairs, and a water dispenser. The seats had been removed, and in their place was a bus stop bench that looked like they had taken it off the street. On the opposite wall was a receptionist area separated by glass paneling. We went up to it, cautiously.

There was no-one behind the receptionist's window, nor chairs, nor desks or computers. Just a single pendant lightbulb illuminating the abandoned receptionist area. Taped to the glass was a piece of printer paper with a message written in black marker:

> RING ONCE FOR SERVICES,
> THREE TIMES FOR THE MANAGERIAL SPECIAL.

I looked at Greg, then saw that to the left of the window, next to a knobless door, was a small buzzer. Greg reached for it and rung it three times. Electric whirring sounded from the other side.

Just as I'd begun to think that no one was here, a door opened. I could hear it somewhere behind the wall. Behind the window, a lineup of six women stood in formation in the receptionist area. They appeared to be strippers. They wore various outfits: nurse, schoolgirl, French maid, and a leather-clad cat. All of them were remarkably ugly women. We're talking like twos here. Squalid, bucktoothed, asymmetric eyes, tramp stamps, under-boob tattoos, stretch marks, back hair. A veritable Mount Rushmore for pitiable genetics and poor life choices.

"Oh, this seems promising," said Greg. Before I could respond with a "let's get the fuck out of here," a maître d' emerged—a short Asian woman wielding an English riding crop.

"Have you decided?" she said from behind the window. Her back was turned to us as she inspected her lineup like a staff sergeant at drill.

"Oooh, tough choice," Greg said, resting his head on his hand like a Rodin statue. "Uh, who ya gonna go with?" He looked sideways at me, studying the display like he was some kind of art afficionado at the Met.

"You know, it's tough but… probably no one. But you go crazy in there." I stood next to him as he deliberated.

Greg eventually pointed at the taller, not-pregnant-looking one in the nurse's uniform. The girls went back behind whatever door they'd come out of. A short time later, a lock clicked, and the knobless door ominously opened. Greg flashed me the deuces, then disappeared into the dark portal. The door shut and locked behind him. I sat on the bus stop bench and listened for screaming or any other indication that Greg was being murdered; if I heard anything, I would run and call the cops. No way was I about to play hero.

While I waited, a young man, likely a private, came in looking quite skittish. His eyes widened when he saw me sitting on the bench.

"D-D'you work here?" he said.

"Yeah, but my shift is over… I'm not doing any more dances tonight, pal," I said.

"Oh, hahaha… are you a cop?" Before I could even answer, he

was out the door and getting into a vehicle. I was beginning to wonder how I'd never heard of this place before.

Later, Greg emerged.

"You all good?"

"Yeah, let's go on and get out of here."

"What happened in there?"

"I'll tell you when we're in the car."

Turns out the story wasn't all that interesting. He went back to a private room, probably formerly a dentist's office. His girl closed a door and gave him a price sheet that consisted of "extra services." I can't remember the prices he told me exactly, but some surprising things were concerningly cheap. The good news was that despite just busting a nut, he was down to party, so we headed to our next stop: the Velvet Mirage.

The Velvet Mirage is the quintessential military strip club: it's large, makes way too much money, and has become something of a mascot for the township itself. It was Wednesday, so they had wings and one-dollar shots, according to their sign outside. We went in, paid our much more reasonably priced cover charge, and made our way over to the bar. Girls were dancing; since they had teeth and no visible deformities, I deemed it a Grade A establishment. We got some beers and played pool until a busty waitress came around and asked if we wanted two-dollar titty shots.

Since I was DD, I declined, but Greg eagerly accepted. The busty waitress pushed Greg down on a chair and gave him a brief lap dance. She then pulled out a shot in a long glass test tube from the tray she carried and somewhat sexily deep-throated the test tube. She pulled it out and then placed the test tube between her breasts and had him take the shot from there. Greg ordered five more.

I wound up playing pool by myself while Greg took shots. He briefly took a break and went to a backroom for a semi-private lap dance. When he returned, he did more breast shots from the server. Greg was feeling pretty lit when a pretty girl came by offering a lap dance. Greg encouraged me to go back with her. Being a man of culture, I obliged.

The back room was lined with red felt and consisted of cushy couches in rows with every other couch flipped so that it faced the couch behind it. It was dark and moody, with a faintly strobing disco ball, and also empty. The stripper took off her top, revealing perky nipples and a tattooed torso. She then straddled me and lap-danced with conviction, which I was fine with. But then she had to stand up turn around and put her ass in my face, which would've been great if weren't for a serious case of the swamp-ass. The reason I know this is because she buried my face into her ass—nose to asshole—and I got a very good whiff. I was once again concerned that a stripper had given me pink eye. I backed my head away trying to get some air and pushed her ass away from me.

"No touching!" she warned, and waggled a finger at me, then proceeded to push her ass into my face once again. I was getting tea bagged by a stripper. The music was loud, and her grody ass was muffling my voice. She couldn't hear me asking her to stop. I endured several minutes of this until I finally got her attention. I tapped a stupid Seed of Life tattoo she had on her ass and asked her about it. She immediately plopped down next to me.

"You know what that is?" Her dim eyes sparkled with delight.

"Oh, do I," I said, very glad that her ass was out of my face. We proceeded to have an all too lengthy and (to me) wildly uninteresting conversation about sacred geometry. It became very clear to me that she was on the market and looking for a Joe with Tricare. Thankfully, she did not charge me, and instead just stole thirty minutes of my life. Funny enough, this stripper would reappear in my life in the form of another soldier's wife.

I returned to the main room to go find a bathroom to wash my face, then I returned to the club. Greg was doing another shot from the waitress chick, who now seemed way too into the boob shots and deep throating test tubes. I glanced at the time and saw that it was getting late. I gathered Greg up and we headed back to base.

◆

Greg was pretty drunk but mostly coherent. We got back onto base and into our barracks rooms… no problem. I made sure that he set several alarms on his phone so he wouldn't miss formation in the morning. It wasn't too late, only around six p.m., if I remember correctly. I took off, heading to the chow hall to indulge in DFAC delicacies.

I was poking at a mystery casserole when I got the text.
"Hey man, I'm not feeling too well," texted Greg.
"Pukey?" I asked.
"Nah man, I just feel weird."
"Weird how?"
I saw that he was typing away. It seemed like he was writing an elaborate description. Some time passed, and he continued to type.

Ten minutes later, he still hadn't responded. Starting to get worried, I pondered what kind of pink wiggly meat was in the casserole. I reckoned it was probably some sort of off-brand Spam or canned liver.

"So, ya feeling okay?" I sent. Fifteen minutes later, there was still no response, and now I was starting to get really worried. "Yo Greg, give me a status update so I know you're good."

I was no longer interested in attempting to eat my meal. I threw the food into the garbage—where it belonged—and headed out the DFAC and towards my car. I called Greg.
RING
RING
RING
Nothing. I decided that I needed to go check on my dude.

A short while later, and after several ignored phone calls, I knocked on Greg's door. No response. I pressed my ear to the door to see if I can hear him inside, listening for any signs of activity. I checked my phone and saw that he still hasn't responded. "Shit." I pounded on Greg's door. The walls between rooms in the quad around me were shaking. "Hey! Greg! You in there! Open up!" I yelled.

A door to the room to my left opened, and a wide-eyed private, whom I recognized, peered out of his hole like a scared prairie dog.

"Hey you!" I said. He tensed up a bit, obviously still unsure if I was cadre or an NCO.

"Y—yes?" he said.

"Have you seen Greg? Do you know if he's left or not?"

"Uhh, no clue," he said, sensing I was low threat.

"How about his roommate? Do you know who he is or have his number?" I said.

"He doesn't have one. The lucky bastard…"

"Well, this has been amazingly unhelpful," I said.

I started pounding and shouting at Greg's door again. The timid private took this as his cue to dip back into his hole. This went on for some time, and I began to deliberate my next move. I didn't know what was wrong with Greg. The last text I got from him read, "I just feel weird," which did not bode well, especially since he was now unresponsive. He'd done a lot of shots; I wasn't even sure how many, to be frank. I began to imagine that my friend was in there, passed out and choking to death on his vomit. Images of musicians chortling to death in the prime of their lives came to mind. I knew I had to get in. I took a few steps back and charged the door.

One moment I was dominating a point of entry, the next I was on my back seeing stars. My shoulder and my head hurt righteously. But more than anything else, I was stunned. The Army that issued me disintegrating boots, the Army that issued me hydrophilic rain jackets, the Army that issued ear plugs that caused hearing loss, the Army that had cancer water, lead-based face paint, asbestos blankets, etcetera, etcetera, had managed to get one fucking thing right. They built a motherfucking solid ass door that not even Jean Claude Van Damme could kick in.

This fucker was all steel, double dead-bolted, in a steel frame, bedded in concrete. Up until this time, I'd always wondered what the Department of Defense did with their massive fucking budget. Because they didn't spend it on quality equipment, food, or healthy living conditions, and certainly not on morale. I realized that I was gonna have to get a room key to get in. But the question was, from where?

I remembered that the CQ desk could provide me with a key to get into a room. They would have to escort me and let me in though. I hoped to God someone I knew would be attending the desk.

It was someone I knew. It was uppity duppity, uptight wannabe SSG, SGT Rork, whom everyone called Rork the Dork.

"Hey, I need to get into my room," I said.
"You can start by addressing me as sergeant and from the position of parade rest," the nasally SGT Rork said. I was not in uniform, as it was around seven p.m. on a Wednesday. Though both of his requests were bullshit, I didn't want to invite any more trouble to an already troubled situation, so I complied.

"That's better, now how can I help you?" He enunciated every word very obnoxiously.

"Sergeant, I need to get into my room," I said.

"Okay, what's your room number?"

"119," I said. He opened the key book log, and searched for the room number, then traced his finger over to the list of corresponding names.

"Your name isn't listed for this room," he said. The clock was ticking in my head. Greg might very well be dead in his room, so I cut the crap to try and expedite this process.

"Sergeant, I have reason to think that my friend may be passed out or having some sort of health issue in his room. I do not know for sure, but I got a mysterious text from him, and want to check and see if he is alright," I said.

He looked at me, a bit stunned. But thankfully, he nodded his head and grabbed the key ring. We moved quickly up to Greg's room. We spent a painful amount of time outside of Greg's room as SGT Rork, tried to figure out which fucking key went to this particular door. After about fifteen tries, we got in. As soon as the door swung open, I burst inside, and there Greg was, standing in the middle of his room in his boxers like a jackass.

Just when I was about to start chewing him out, he wobbled, buckled, and then stumbled towards me. It was the second zombie charge I'd experienced that day. He grabbed onto me and muttered incoherently. His eyes seemed to roll around in his head. I saw that he was not fine. I grabbed him and sat him down on his bed forcefully. Opening his fridge to see if there was anything in there with electrolytes, I found two unopened bottles of Gatorade, cracked open a frost white one, and tried to make him drink it. He made loose eye contact with me as he did so. I had to hold it for him like I was bottle-feeding a newborn. Gatorade spilled down his face and onto the front of his boxers.

"Uhh uggaa ujhhhh jmamama Joeeeeeeeeyy," he said. SGT Rork stood there watching as I waterboarded Greg.

"Look, clearly your friend's fucked up. There might be an issue here. I'm going to call this in."

"Call it in... like an ambulance?"

"No, I'm going to report it to our cadre," he said. Rork the Dork was about to call up our cadre, late on a weekday. Our cadre was going to leave his family (assuming they weren't divorced) and drive back to base to deal with a soldier who'd decided to get drunk at a strip club. I knew my ass might fry for this too.

"Sergeant, do you really think that is necessary?" I said. But his ear was already to the phone and connecting with one of our cadre. He held up a finger to silence me. Rork called it in, like one of Hitler's Youths. I wondered if Rork had the cadre on speed dial.

A while later, the cadre knocked on the door. Then three very pissed off green berets came inside. They looked at me, then at Greg, and at me again.

"What the fuck happened?" SFC Magnus asked. I stood up and went to parade rest.

"Sergeant, we went to a strip club. I was his DD, drove him back here. He seemed fine when I left him. But then I got a text from him saying that he felt weird. After sending that message he did not respond to my replies, nor answer my calls. I was worried about him. I came to the room and knocked on his door and didn't get a response. So I informed SGT Rork of the situation and he got a key and got us into the room, and I've been trying to rehabilitate him." Greg did finally seem to be coming to his senses a bit better. He was averting eye contact with the SFC.

"Hey, fuck head," SFC Magnus said, "this is why you don't fucking drink on a fucking weeknight." He glared at Greg, who was still clearly disoriented.

"What strip club did ya'll go to?" Magnus asked.

I told him. SFC Magnus looked to the other cadre. He motioned for his subordinate to inspect Greg. SSG Steele, presumably an 18D, knelt in front of Greg and instructed him to follow his fingertip with his eyes, then checked his pupils out with a flashlight.

"Yeah, did you see anything get put into one of his drinks?" SSG Steele asked. I shook my head.

"He seems to be coming down off of whatever it is. Could just be low electrolytes," said SSG Steele.

"Joe, keep an eye on him. I expect to see both of you at tomorrow's formation, 0630 sharp," SFC Magnus said.

"Roger that," I said. Just like that the green beret cadre left, as did SGT Rork, who shook his head and sneered at us as he left. I stayed with Greg a while longer, nursing him back to normalcy.

About an hour later he seemed to come to his senses and didn't remember much of what had transpired. I recounted the events to him.

"Oh, fuck!" Greg said.

SFC Magnus smoked us pretty bad the next day, but that is as far as the issue ever went. Greg would live to fight another day.

BAILING AND RAILING

This story occurred while I was a Special Forces Candidate.
A buddy of mine, Ralph, a guy I'd known since Basic, had come into the Army as an 18x. Right away everyone could tell that he'd made a mistake. He was a doughy, anime-watching, woke liberal from somewhere in the Northeast. He struggled to fit in at infantry bootcamp, but I liked him all the same. It had been a while since I'd seen him; he'd disappeared one weekend due to some mysterious emergency. So it surprised me when I got a phone call from him.

"Hey, Joe. It's Ralph. How's it going?" he said.

"It's going good, Ralph, how about you?" I said.

"Yeah, so it's been going man… look… something crazy happened this weekend," he said.

"Do I even want to know?" I asked.

"Probably not, but anyways there's this girl, we're friends, her name is Chloe, and anyhow Friday night I got a phone call from her. She was in trouble. In jail and needed someone to come bail her out. So I got my stuff, and drove up to New Jersey, and I paid her bail."

I processed all of this. "Yup, checks out. No red flags whatsoever," I said.

"Anyway, we've been hanging out, and now we're a… kinda thing. So I'm coming back down and figured we could spend the four-day weekend at my parents' beach house down in Outer Banks. I've invited Greg and Austin to come along with. You down?" he asked.

"Yeah, man, shoot me the address and me and Greg will head on down together. I appreciate the invite, dude. Look forward to hanging... and meeting the lady," I said.

I hurried to pack a weekend bag, grabbing swim trunks, sunscreen, condoms, candy—you know, the essentials. I got my shit, gave Greg a call, and told him to hurry up.

Pretty soon we were on our way.

Early in our drive down to Outer Banks, Greg had asked me about some movie. I said that I hadn't seen it, and he proceeded to give me his review.

"You know, I'm something of a movie buff," he said.

I nodded, sensing that this conversation had taken a strongly autistic turn. "Oh, that's cool man," I said, not really wanting to wade into this particular topic further. When he reached for the volume knob and turned down the radio, I knew I was fucked.

"What's your favorite movie?" he asked. Indeed, the conversation had gone full autistic.

"Ummm... you know... I'm not really—"

"Great," he interrupted "My favorite movie is *The Good, the Bad and the Ugly*... let me explain."

Greg then went on a thirty minute monologue explaining why he thought it was such an excellent film, going into detail about the cinematography and casting, and he even went so far as to recreate entire scenes for me, which I begrudgingly admit were pretty well done.

I did consider swerving into several light poles though.

Greg and I arrived in the Outer Banks. We drove through an expensive-looking neighborhood until we arrived at an impressive three-story home, only about a block back from the beach.

"Yo, this place looks tight," said Greg.

"It sure does," I responded, trying to determine if the three-story drop would be enough to kill Greg. Around the same time, Austin arrived in his red compact SUV, which can best be described as a chick car.

"What's up, my niggas?" said the large Black Texan. He was wearing a pair of flashy Pit Vipers. All the military guys thought they were the coolest thing. I never got a pair.

Austin joined Greg and me, and we went up the stairs to go meet up with Ralph. We walked in through the garage with our luggage and saw that we had both a staircase and an elevator to choose between. We felt like we were in the Taj Mahal.

"What the fuck do Ralph's parents do?" Austin asked.

"I don't know. Wall Street or something," Greg said as we clamored into the elevator and went up to the third floor. The elevator doors opened up to a large room with an open floor plan. There were balconies on both sides of a large open-concept common area that had a ping-pong table, refrigerator, bar, and a surround sound stereo system blasting. Ralph stood there in a Hawaiian shirt, dancing alone. He turned around and saw us. Fist bumps were exchanged.

"So, where's the new lady, my dude?" I asked.

"Oh, she's not here yet. She's coming down with her roommates later," he responded. Greg, Austin and I grinned; 'roommates' sounded like a good time to us.

"So tell me about these roommates..." Greg inquired. "We talking single? Fat? Hot? Hot and Fat?"

"Yeah, what are we working with here, nigga?" Austin exclaimed, throwing down some gangster signs as he did so.

"Ummm, actually, they're guys." He laughed and gave us the eye, like maybe we would be into that. "But yes, they are single."

"Wait... she's roommates with a bunch of dudes?" Austin asked.

"Umm, yeah, one of them is an ex of hers, but he seems real nice so I invited him too," Ralph casually responded. This caused me to slap my head; that didn't sound like a good idea at all to me. We all had so many questions but for the time being, kept our mouths shut.

"She's super-hot though, y'all are gonna love her. She's *crazy* in bed, too. Ahahahaha! Alright, lemme show ya'll to your rooms, and you can get settled."

It turned out the three of us had to share a room. Which was… whatever. We stowed our stuff into some drawers and shifted our bags under the beds. Once settled, we immediately began to speculate about this new girl of his.

"So to recap, this is some girl who got arrested for attacking police officers, who Ralph bailed out of jail and is now dating. She has two roommates, both of whom are dudes, one of whom is her ex?" Greg said in a quick recap.

"That's what I'm tracking," I said.

"Damn, nigga," Austin said, still wearing his pit vipers. We heard a door slam and people clomping around a short time later.

"I guess she's here. C'mon guys, we should go introduce ourselves." We marched out of the room and called for the elevator, eager to see the train wreck that awaited us on the next floor.

The doors parted, and Ralph was dancing around with his new friends. There were two skinny looking dudes, dressed like the goth kids from South Park. Replete with facial piercings and long hair, they starkly contrasted the three clean-cut military bros who had just come on deck. Now the star of the show, Chloe, turned around. She was a rail thin, pale, vaguely sick-looking fe-male, with a bull ring nose piercing. Based on her appearance and yellowed teeth, I deduced that she was a druggy.

Austin peered over his Pit Vipers and gave me a quick sideways glance. Clearly, he had the same realization as I did. I nodded to him, and we kept our mouths shut.

"Hi, you must be Chloe," Greg said. "Ralph has been telling us so much about you."

I thanked God that Greg was so loquacious. Chloe looked him up and down, then eyed all of us, like a butcher trying to grade meat. Her eyes hovered over me, she smiled, and stared at my crotch—all right in front of Ralph, who walked up beside her and grabbed her ass, like a true romantic.

"Glad to see ya'll have finally met. This is Chloe, guys," he said chummily.

"Hey Chloe!" Austin and I said in chorus.

"Ralph, how about you start getting some drinks going so we can get this party started?" Chloe said.

"Yeah, what time do the clubs open?" asked one of the emo guys. I think his name was Favian or something stupid.

"Oh, yeah, we could definitely use a drink," I said. I went with Ralph over to the next room to get something very strong.

We all got busy drinking. Austin and I repeatedly tried to strike up conversations with Ralph, Chloe, and her emo entourage. She became increasingly flirty. At one point, she disappeared downstairs with her "ex-boyfriend" only to reemerge much later looking a bit disheveled. Ralph seemed either oblivious to or didn't care; I wasn't sure which. Austin and I knew we needed to talk to him. Greg, on the other hand, was getting along famously with Chloe and her entourage, and he was getting pretty hammered. We tried but failed to get Ralph to step outside with us for a quick chat. He refused, saying he was needed for this or that. So Austin and I did what any self-respecting twenty-something-year-olds would do. We did some shots, grabbed a beer, and went looking for Pokémon on the beach.

For those of you who might not remember, Pokémon Go was at one point all the rage. The Pokémon Go fever had swept across

Fort Bragg, wreaking havoc. Several locations on base were known to be rare Pokémon hotspots. Military vehicles had been wrecked, formations broken, people run over, secret compounds infiltrated, and lot of fights had broken out as a result, effectively reducing Fort Bragg to a state of anarchy. If this was a Japanese plot to subvert American military might, it was working stupendously. Needless to say, Austin and I had likewise been compromised.

While drunk and strolling the beach, we searched for the Pokémon, or something to that effect. Admittedly, my memory of this event, like most others in this book, is a bit blurry at best. But somehow or another, he wound up tackling me into the ocean. Then I grabbed him and tackled him into the ocean.

Somewhere along the way he realized he'd lost his wallet, with all of his credit cards, money, and military IDs. Needless to say, this ruined both his and my night. We combed the beach, but it was beginning to get dark, so we decided to head back to the beach house with our tails tucked between our legs, sandy, and down a wallet.

We took the elevator to the top and looked for the rest of the crew. We heard music playing on the outside deck. We did a couple of shots, grabbed some beers, and went out to join them. We slid open the deck to the outside, and there they were, all of them butt-ass naked. Four dudes, one girl, some sitting some standing, all butt-ass naked. Austin and I about dropped our drinks.

"What the fuuu…" I said.

"Yay! You're here," Chloe said, getting up and hugging me. "Now why don't you two strip down, then we'll play a game."

"What game, nigga?" Austin said.

"So you're all gonna fuck me… then in nine months we're gonna see who the daddy is! I call it Baby Roulette!" Chloe said.

My jaw dropped. I turned to Ralph, who seemed completely unfazed. I looked over at Greg, who quickly crossed his legs. We made eye contact, awkwardly.

"Well… I'm down to play," Greg said.

I just shook my head. There was no way I was going into that girl without a shot of penicillin. "Yeah, Austin and I are gonna get changed real quick. And we'll let ya know," I said as I began backing my way inside with Austin. The naked Chloe just stood there, staring us down. She noticed me noticing her nipple piercings and she smiled devilishly. I slid the door closed, then we hightailed it down the stairs; we did not take the elevator.

"Bro... what the fuck was that?" Austin said.

"I don't know, man, that chick is fucking all kinds of weird," I said. "And what the fuck is up with Ralph?"

"We gotta get the fuck out of here," he said.

"Yeah man, we totally do... but at the same time, I'm kinda wondering how this is gonna play out."

"What the fuck do you mean?"

"I mean, is Ralph a swinger? Or does he think this is just some cool nudist hippy shit and she's just joking around?"

"I don't know, man, he did seem pretty out of it."

"We just got to figure out how we're gonna be getting out of this for tonight."

"We're gonna need to rescue Greg first, though," he said.

"I'm not sure if Greg wants to be rescued."

"We need to, man... no telling what she'll give him."

"Shit..." I began scouring my brain for a way to get out of here with Greg in tow. I got out my phone and began looking at clubs in the area, seeing if any of them were within walking distance.

"There's a club down the ways that's open until two. We could head over that way."

"Aight, lemme just get my clubbing clothes on."

Austin emerged sometime later wearing a brown polo tucked into beige cargo pants, a pair of camouflage Crocs, and long white tube socks, and still rocking the Pit Vipers. He looked like a roided-out eight-year-old whose mom had just dressed him for redneck church.

We were ready. Now we just had to rescue Greg, who was not responding to our texts, probably because his phone was in his pants pocket, which of course, he was not wearing. We were facing a dilemma, and we weren't sure how we were going to accomplish our mission. We moved towards the stairwell and the elevator. We heard giggling and laughter coming from upstairs, and Chloe screaming about something.

I turned towards Austin and said, "Or... we could just go." He shook his head vigorously and pulled his Pit Vipers down so he could look over them and make eye contact with me.

"We never leave a man behind, nigga," Austin said. He righted his sunglasses and went up the stairs. This was the moment I knew Austin would become a Medal of Honor recipient. He went up the stairs alone—I did not follow. I heard a door slide, some more giggling, then some screeching. A short while later, Austin came pulling a butt-ass naked Greg down the stairs by the arm.

"No, man, I want to stay," Greg said.

"Shut up, nigga, and put on some clothes. We going to the club," Austin said. I averted my eyes from Greg's dick as he stood at the base of the stairs, pouting and rubbing his arm where Austin had gripped him. He sulked off into his room, and I heard more commotion upstairs.

"Greg, hurry up, before they try to come with us—"

"Where do you guys think you're going?" A trill, angry voice sounded from the top of the stairs.

I turned to see standing at the top of the staircase, our pale, nude Chloe.

"You know, we're just thinking about going out for some fresh air, maybe checking out a bar or two," I said. Chloe stood there, bristling. I could see the anger fomenting behind her dark eyes. I averted my gaze, actively trying not to look directly at her vulva or any part of her at all. Didn't want to encourage her. A heavy, asphyxiating cloud spread out from her, silencing us into a frozen stupor. Now I've faced down some badass dudes, but this chick was something else altogether.

"Ooh, ya'll trying to go pick up some chicks then?" She laughed cynically, clearly forcing a smile, which reminded me of the doll Chucky from Child's Play.

"Uh, you know the thought did cross our minds," I managed to stammer out. Her smile disappeared. Just as I thought she was about to snap, Ralph came strolling over. His horse-cock swinging for everyone to see.

"Oh, hey what you guys up to?" he said, as he slapped Chloe's ass. Now me and Austin rapidly tried to avert our gaze; the only ones who seemed comfortable with the situation was the two of them, and Greg.

"Yeah, thinking about checking out the bars, you know, get some fresh air and stuff," I said. I didn't want to insult the dude by telling him that his girlfriend was a real freak who was creeping us out.

"Awesome! We'll come with you!" Ralph said. He turned and bellowed, "Hey, Hayden, Favian! Get some clothes on! We're going to the club."

Some muddled whiny sounds came from upstairs.

"What?" Ralph bellowed a huge belly laugh. "We can resume this later. Come on, ya guys!" He gave another strange laugh. I wondered what he thought was so funny.

I turned to Austin, and he just shook his head ever so slightly. I guessed we would be bringing the entourage with us.

The clubs in the area were not what I was expecting. They were full of families and geriatrics, with a smattering of random girls here or there. Chloe stuck to me like glue, having opted to wear cheap Mickey Mouse flip flops, a crop-top without a bra, and extra trashy jorts. She remained close to me at all times and kept trying to get us all drinks. Favian and Hayden eagerly accepted her drinks and found a dark corner to sit in and do emo stuff. Ralph just got progressively drunker and kept laughing long past the point of being fucking annoying. Austin approached various women in his tube socks, Crocs, cargo pants, tucked in shirt, and Pit Vipers. He seemed to be generating some interest.

"Have you heard about our lord and savior, redneck Jesus?" I imagined something to that effect was his pickup line. I frankly wasn't sure if I wanted to be associated with him, or anyone else in our group, for that matter.

I tried talking to some females, but I kept getting cockblocked by Chloe, who guarded me from other females like an eel defending its lair. I was getting fed up.

Austin saw that I was having issues and came up alongside me at the bar. Chloe had just walked off and had left another drink next to me, which I passed along to some rando.

"She's getting everyone fucked up, nigga," Austin said.

"I know, and I don't think she's had anything to drink," I said.

"She wants us drunk and vulnerable so she can have her way with us... all of us. There's something seriously demented about that woman," he said, "and not in a good way."

"I don't know... she's like a vampire who constantly needs fresh blood," I said.

"She's diabolically slutty, nigga," Austin said.

I nodded, then watched Ralph waterfall a drink off her thigh. "How about we start feeding her drinks?" I said.

"Go ahead, I'm listening." Austin leaned in.

"Alright, so maybe we can get her shitfaced, and she'll either be too shitfaced to notice we disappeared, or she'll attack a cop or something and she can get thrown in jail for the weekend," I said. Now we had a plan. I waved for the bartender to come over.

"Alright, so guys in my group want to do shots, but they're a little drunk so I was wondering if you could water down like two of the shots and leave the others normal." I slid a twenty across the bar. This was a very cheap bar.

"You got it, boss. You want well?"

"Yeah, the cheapest grossest shit you got," I said. The bartender smirked, then got cracking on our drinks. I turned to Austin. "I want to put them all out of commission. A nasty hangover should give us a bit more freedom to maneuver."

We brought some shots over and convinced Chloe to begin

taking them with us. Austin and I grabbed the severely watered-down shots and initiated the toast. "To a fun night and to Chloe for getting out of jail! Whooo!" First one went down. Chloe was smiling, reveling in the attention. I made sure to provide plenty of encouragement and positive reinforcement to keep her happy and drinking.

"Alright, to Ralph and his beautiful new girlfriend, Chloe! Whooo!" They all clinked plastic cups and we downed our shots. Austin smirked at me. Chloe seemed to be getting extra horny now, and I was worried that this had backfired. She began suggesting we go back to the beach house. "No, it'll be more fun if we wait." I winked at her, and she smiled devilishly. I ordered more shots.

"Alright, to a great night in the Outer Banks!" Chloe grabbed my ass very aggressively.

"And to Ralph's giant sausage!" Greg said. Everyone laughed. Ralph, Hayden, and Favian were all pretty drunk already, but I could see that Chloe was only a bit buzzed, and still in full-on sexual predator mode. I realized that it would take substantially more to put down the cum-sucking vampire. I went back and got more shots, with all but hers watered down. More rounds were had; Austin and Greg were on the same page as me and each went and got another round of modified shots.

After many more shots, we were all starting to feel it, even though ours had been watered down. Chloe, amazingly, was still standing.

More shots. *How the fuck is she still standing?*

Even more shots. Chloe had become extra frenetic. She was aggressively fondling any ass that came within arm's reach.

"She's gotta be on drugs, what ya think?" I said.

"She's got fucking shark eyes, bro. Oh God, she's looking at me!!" Austin said.

More shots… this wasn't fun anymore.

"Daht woman ain't naturaall—that bitch is possessed or something," the normally teetotaling Austin slurred.

"Yup, like a white trash succubus," Greg said.

"Yeah, man, this isn't looking good. We can't go home this drunk with her. She'll take advantage of poor Austin," I said.

"Agreed... more shots?" Greg said.

"We've got to see it through to the end," Austin said.

Finally, Chloe sat down. It seems that she was finally down for the count. Soon we'd send her, Ralph, Favian, and Damian in an Uber back to the house, and we would finally be able to enjoy our night out.

I felt bony fingers dig into my forearm. I turned to find Chloe's black eyes staring at me intently. "Hey! Chloe!" An ophidian smile unfurled across her face. Her dilated pupils and fangs dripped with salacious intent. I panicked. "You know, Chloe, I think Austin wants to dance with you."

She turned on him like a viper. "Ooh, let's go! You look like a sexy Sunday school boy." They made quite the scene as she grabbed him by the collar and tried to drag him to the dance floor. Austin wouldn't budge.

"Help me!" he begged us.

"It's too late for him," Greg said.

"Wanna sneak out and go to another bar?" I said.

"I sure do," Greg said.

As we walked out, we knew Austin was doing spin moves and refusing to go back to the dance floor with Chloe. But the vampire was relentless. She cut him off at every angle. She had given up on bringing him to the dance circle and aggressively backed her boney ass into him, forcibly twerking on him. Austin had gone down like a hero, enabling Greg and me to escape Chloe's venereal clutches.

We texted him our location, and later he egressed and rendezvoused with us at another bar.

Chloe had lost our trail.

The three of us stayed out very late that night reveling in our newfound freedom and telling tales of the devil bitch from hell.

UNSOLICITED RANT ABOUT THE 82ND AIRBORNE

This is an educational aside.

The 82nd Airborne Division is comprised of special operations duds and leadership whose IQs were too low to even attend a spec ops selection. So you get a combination of the saltiest dudes on the planet, mixed in with people who are dumb enough to think Airborne is still relevant. This mixture is pretty toxic as it turns out. To compensate for being less than special operations, the 82nd Airborne Division's leadership substitutes cool training, and personal time with formations—they love them. Let me explain.

There's a 6:15 a.m. PT-formation for morning physical training, where we stand in formation in the dark and listen to the reverie. After this formation, we then move into smaller formations for normal PT events, and occasionally larger battalion-sized formations for big group runs. Once PT is complete, we dissolve out of these formations and move into what is known as a release-formation. After release-formation, there is sometimes a post-release formation with your platoon leader, where he will tell us about all the other formations they've got on the books for the day before releasing us for breakfast.

After breakfast, we arrive promptly at the motor pool to once again stand in formation. Then there's sometimes a formation after lunch, occasionally one between lunch and final formation, then finally a final-formation, which sometimes isn't the actual final-formation, and is instead a formation to notify you that the actual final-formation has been pushed back. Then at the final-final-formation, they tell us to be prepared for a recall-formation. After final-final-formation, company leadership puts you into a formation to inform you of the additional formations that need to happen in the event there's a battalion-recall-formation.

The company commander usually cooks up some brilliant plan to have a pre-battalion-recall-formation-formation, to ensure they squared away everything for the battalion commander. Then the platoon LTs plan a pre-pre-battalion-recall-formation-formation so that they can make sure they squared away everything for the company commander. Subsequently, the NCOIC will insist on a pre-pre-pre-battalion-recall-formation-formation-formation to ensure we avoid pissing off the LTs at the subsequent pre-pre-battalion-recall-formation-formation.

But formations aren't always a bad thing! Sometimes, to celebrate rewards and build morale, the 82nd will organize an award-ceremony-formation, where we can watch someone get a medal for not getting a DUI or domestic abuse charge in over three years. This is referred to as a Good Conduct Medal. They then give a speech about this remarkable achievement.

I'm sure to someone not in the military this sounds a bit ridiculous, and it is. But don't think for a second that these formations only occur while not at war. No! The 82nd brass is so committed to formations, they do them everywhere. I have many vivid memories of standing in formation, in the middle of a base that was frequently the target of mortar and rocket attacks, because some lieutenant colonel enjoyed having a captive audience.

Some of the best years of my life were squandered standing in formations.

But the formations are just one aspect of life in the 82nd. Everyone hates each other, alcoholism is rampant, you get no free time, and there are endless details and training-related fatalities—more on this in a bit. Remember the definition of the Green Weenie I provided in an earlier chapter?

Well, nowhere else is the malevolence of the Green Weenie more concentrated than in the 82nd Airborne. The leadership has famously little regard for their soldiers. I've experienced them not letting anyone go home for days until a $200 piece of equipment is found because someone in another unit lost one, or disapproving leave for soldiers who are newlyweds, new fathers, or trying to attend a family member's funeral. If you get smart on them and try to leave, they'll deliberately stall or concoct some bullshit reason not to approve packets for career advancement, or soldiers looking to go try out for special operations. If you somehow manage to run the packet up the command and get it signed, I pity you.

The 82nd leadership will stick you on a twenty-four-hour detail the night before going to an arduous selection, to sabotage your chances—true story, it happened to me. Not to mention my 1SG came by every day to tell me I was a pussy and wouldn't make it.

Perhaps what best epitomizes the 82nd is the DONSA. A DONSA is a day off that is awarded to the entire 82nd Airborne when the division goes eighty-two consecutive days without a training fa-tality. There is a red neon sign along Gruber (or was), that shows the number of days since the last training fatality. I have never seen that number make it past twenty. The joke is, if the number gets high enough, the command orders up a bunch of combat night jumps (which are notoriously dangerous training exer-cises).

For these reasons, smart people tend to get the fuck out of the 82nd Airborne. Now, because all the smart, competent people leave, what remains are the most toxic and incompetent individuals. These are the people who rise in the hierarchy and become the leaders of tomorrow, so the organization becomes increasingly toxic.

THE COCK BLOCK

One weekend while I was in the 82nd, it was rumored that the Sergeant Major and the Battalion Commander were gone on a fishing trip, which might have had something to do with the fact that we had a three-day weekend on the schedule. Currently, there were no recall formations anticipated, nor was I slated for a twenty-four-hour weekend CQ duty; no details were being meted out, no mandatory battalion pow-wows, no field training exercises were going on, and we weren't on twelve-hour recall status. It seemed the stars had finally aligned, and that I would get a three-day weekend. How could this be?

Like the angel of death passing over the blood-painted doors during the Passover, the Green Weenie, it seemed, had shown us favor. This was a rare occurrence, one that I was keen to take advantage of.

I hit up an old friend I'd made while in Airborne Holdover, a Hispanic kid named Ricardo. He'd been around Fort Bragg longer, so I figured that he would know about places to have a good time. I knew he needed it; I'd been a bit worried about him. He was having a miserable time at his new unit: the 82nd Airborne Division. [If you are unfamiliar with the 82nd Airborne, please read "Unsolicited Rant about the 82nd Airborne."]

Ricardo was an especially disgruntled soldier. Every time I talked to him, he would complain about his unit. To be fair, he did seem to get fucked over by the unit frequently. They were always putting him on details, writing him up on pretenses, and engaging him in "training exercises" that involved zero training and lots of broken-ass Humvees. Couldn't blame him. I was pretty fed up with this division's bullshit too. So this weekend, the first weekend we'd had in months, we decided to head on down to Myrtle Beach to hit up some bars and hit on some chicks. Going into it, we both cleaned up well, Ricardo especially being the suave blue-eyed Hispanic man that he is. Chicks always digged him. I knew he was going to be a great wingman.

We hit the bars, and pretty quickly Ricardo chatted up two chicks. He waved me over. The conversation seemed to be going pretty well, and eventually, the girls invited us over to their place for a few drinks. We gladly agreed, got an Uber, and headed over to their place. We'd been drinking a lot already, then we did a few tequila shots at their place. I was talking up the cute blonde, and he had the brunette. *We're set. I'm going to get laid. Life is dandy.* But that last tequila shot did something funky to Ricardo, and the girls began asking us questions about work. We moved over to the couch, and I sat next to my blonde. Ricardo elected to sit on the floor in front of us, which I thought was kind of weird, but decided to not say anything.

"So how is it jumping out of airplanes?" one of the girls asked.

"It's terrible..." Ricardo responded. He just left it like that.

I waited for him to continue before I jumped in. "Well, you know, it's exciting, the adrenaline rush, the energy of it. It beats working in a cubicle." The girls seemed to be eating it up.

"No, no, don't lie to them... it hurts, you're in a hot and overly tight harness that strangles the boys to death." Ricardo gesticulated towards his nut sack. "And you hate your life every second of it."

"Oh my..." the blonde said.

"Yes, but it's worse. Sometimes the place is so horrible and depressing that I hope my parachute doesn't open... I've seen it happen to a few guys. They jump out, the parachute rolls up like a cigarette, and pewwww..." Ricardo demonstrated his hand splatting against the earth. "Lucky bastards." He took another shot of tequila and refilled his glass.

"Haha he's just kidding, ladies. There is a little bit of danger in it, but you know, that's what makes you feel alive," I said.

"I'm not exaggerating. We have a sign in the 82nd that tracks how many days the entire division has gone without a training fatality. If we do eighty-two days in a row without a dude dying, we get a day off—I've never seen the sign make it past fifteen days." Ricardo downed another shot. "And that's not even counting the guys who check themselves out." Ricardo made a gun with his fingers, put it in his mouth and shot himself in the head for emphasis. "Twenty-two a day."

"Oh my god, that's so depressing," the brunette said.

"Yeah, but the benefits are good, you meet a lot of good people, and we're within driving distance of Myrtle Beach," I said, shooting Ricardo a stern look.

"Oh yeah, do you guys come out here often?" the blonde asked.

"No," Ricardo interjected, "We don't because our toxic leadership won't grant us passes. They make it their life's purpose to ensure that our morale remains low."

"Oh my," said the brunette.

I could practically hear their pussies snapping shut like clams. Ricardo kept drinking and seemed to be crying a little bit. He turned to me. "I don't want to go back, man!"

The game was over. The brunette stood up. "Well, it's about our bedtime. How about we call you guys an Uber?"

"Don't make me go back there," Ricardo said.

"We'll just go back to our hotel. Thank you for the drinks, ladies." I got up and took the cockblocker out to the Uber and to the nearest shitty motel. I got us a room since the bars were long past closed.

The next morning, we awoke hungover. While getting breakfast, Ricardo matched with a girl on Tinder. He was in a pretty lousy state, however, and a bit queasy, but I encouraged him to go on the date. I became extra adamant when I found out she would be bringing a friend. He was resistant to the idea, but I hoped that we could maybe still salvage this three-day. He messaged her and she agreed to bring a friend, so we linked up with them on the beach. It turned out the girl Ricardo matched with was quite cute, but—unfortunately for me—her friend was *not*. Additionally, Ricardo was still drunk and very nauseated. I tried to cover up for him and wound up doing most of the talking for him during that date. I even ran interference when he had to dig a hole to puke into. I performed marvelously and charmed the shit out of both his date and her fat friend.

After some time, I realized that I needed to get some greasy food down Ricardo, so I moved the date to a nearby beach bar. We got some food. Ricardo was drunk and could barely converse. The date went fine, and we left.

A year later, Ricardo married that girl. And they stayed married, had kids and shit, and lived happily ever after—mostly.

You see, Ricardo made a serious error in judgment—he thought that things would be a whole lot better if only he were an officer. He decided to go to OCS, and since he wanted to be closer to his girlfriend, he decided to apply to Marian University. The problem was that he didn't apply to the Francis Marian University of South Carolina, but rather to Marian University in Wisconsin. Due to paperwork being filed, and the Army bureaucracy being the beast that it is, he was pretty much stuck going there. Ricardo moved up to Wisconsin.

I didn't see him for years. After graduation, he went back to the same unit that had been the bane of his existence and found that it was even worse as an officer! But now that he had a wife and kids, he was stuck working that gig. My boy fucked up. Every time I've talked to him since he immediately launches into a depressed rant about how awful life is in the 82nd. He Green Weenied himself.

MRS. RIGHT

This story occurred while I was a Special Forces candidate. It was about three in the afternoon on a Saturday. I was fighting off a nasty hangover from the night before when my phone buzzed on the nightstand. Nervously, I checked the caller ID to make sure it wasn't one of my NCOs calling me up for some cruel, impromptu weekend detail. Thankfully it was just my friend Ralph.

"What's up, man?" I answered.

"Hey, Joe, will you be a witness?" I was a bit confused by this question.

"A witness... for what?"

"I'm getting married," Ralph said.

"Oh... yeah, I'll do that," I answered, pretty sure that he had said he was getting married.

"Great! I'm outside the barracks. Meet me down here when you're ready."

"Wait, what... right now?" But he'd already clicked the call closed. "Sick." I closed the call on my end, hurriedly put on shorts, and went downstairs. I wasn't too sure if I needed to dress up for this or not. But given the urgency of the situation and my lack of clothing options, I decided that the T-shirt and shorts would suffice. I wondered who it was that Ralph intended to marry. This question was quickly answered, though, once I spotted the occupant in the passenger seat of his car—the one and only Chloe.

I did a double take. Was Ralph seriously about to marry Chloe? The chick he'd bailed out of prison? The chick who'd cheated on him countless times? The chick who'd gotten naked at a house party and exclaimed, "Everyone fuck me, and then we'll see who the daddy is!"

Anyhow, as I got into the car, he quickly and proudly pronounced that slut-cakes was his bride to be. My mind was fucking blown. On our way to the courthouse, we picked up our second witness, a guy I'd never really hung out with before. He sported a long, dark stain down the front of his shirt and smelled like vomit.

"Couldn't you have put on a clean shirt at least?" I asked.

"Trust me, the rest are far worse," he responded. Sniffing the air, I found that very hard to believe.

"Is that—"

"Yes, it's vomit..." he interjected. "It happened last night." Somehow the fact that it had happened the night before did not make me feel any better about sitting right next to him.

"You shall henceforth be known as Pukestain!" I said to him. With this motley crew, we made our way to the courthouse.

"Is this where the courthouse is at?" I asked, stupefied that we'd just parked outside the town penitentiary.

"Yes, it is," Ralph answered.

"Wow, really fucking romantic, man," I said. Ralph shot me a disapproving look, but Chloe laughed and felt my ass with her hand as she passed. I was becoming uncomfortable with the entire situation.

We made our way through the front entrance, getting scanned and x-rayed by security before navigating through the halls to the courthouse. We opened the door and went to the counter. A frowning geriatric sat behind the Plexiglas.

"What're you here for?" the judge asked.

"To get married," Chloe said.

"Got the paperwork?" the judge said.

"Yes," Ralph said, sliding the paper through the slot. The judge looked it over.

"That will be $15," the judge said. Ralph handed the money over. A door to our left clicked open. "Please proceed to the chapel, where you will be married."

The chapel was a small, dingy space. It was everything I thought a prison chapel would be. The judge came in. They did the vows. When asked, we did not provide any reasons the couple should not marry. It was already self-evident.

"I now pronounce you… man and wife." And just like that, Ralph was a married man.

♦

The wedding posse made its way over to a local bar, where we proceeded to buy the newlyweds a couple of drinks. I'd somehow agreed to being the designated driver. Chloe quickly began knocking them back. Soon she was telling me how great my ass was and repeatedly grabbed it, right in front of her husband. I tried to stay as close to him as I could and kept my ass backed up to the bar whenever she was near.

They had a few more drinks before plans were made for the next stop of the wedding tour. Chloe suggested that we go to the strip club, so we headed to the best strip club in town, the Velvet Mirage.

We got there and were searched for the second time that day, this time by a bouncer. We made our way inside the seedy club, where some stripper halfheartedly went through her routine before unceremoniously discarding her bra like it was a used tissue.

It just so happened that it was one dollar shot night at the club. Like any proper gentleman, I bought the crew a round of drinks. After their first shot, the unenthusiastic stripper approached the table we sat at. She took a seat on Pukestain's lap, straddling him and rubbing her genitals across him. Apparently, she was either unaware of or unconcerned about the vomit on his shirt.

"What brings you to the Velvet Mirage?" she asked the group.

"We just got married!" Chloe said enthusiastically.

"Oh my..." the stripper said, sounding mildly appalled.

"Yeah, and Ralph has never had a lap dance before," Chloe said, nudging Ralph.

"It's okay, Chloe... I'm good," Ralph said.

Chloe ignored his protests and gave the stripper a twenty. "Give Ralph a good time!"

The glum stripper sighed, then grabbed his hand and dragged him into some private room in the back. Once Ralph had disappeared, Chloe went towards the bar and began talking to the manager, who wore a very managerial looking brassiere. The manager handed Chloe some paperwork, which she began to fill out furiously. I ambled over to find out what she was doing.

"What you got there, Chloe?" I asked as candidly as I could.

"Oh, I'm putting in a job application!" she said. On her wedding night.

"Huh..." I made a note of this and returned to my seat. Eventually, Ralph and Chloe returned to the table, at which point they began taking full advantage of one dollar shot night. Six shots later they were all over each other making out. Ralph's hand was making its way down the front of her pants when they suddenly both went still. Their heads clunked. She spilled off of him, her unconscious face now pressed against the dirty carpet of the strip club floor. Ralph was comatose in the chair. The bouncer quickly came over and got in my face.

"You have to get them out of here! We can't have people unconscious in our club!"

"Right, 'cause this is a family establishment, after all," I said.

The bouncer did not appreciate the joke. "Get these two the fuck outta here!" he yelled.

"Alright, alright, I'll handle it." I turned to Pukestain, who was knocking back another shot.

"Hey, we need to get them out of here," I said. He looked up at me, wide-eyed.

"Huhhh?" Pukestain said.

"They're unconscious, help me get them out of here!" I said.

"No, I like… it… here, I don't wanna goo!" Pukestain said. He was incorrigible and drunk.

I knew I was on my own. With a bouncer breathing down my neck, I called an audible and decided to carry each of them out individually to the car. I started with Ralph, whom I threw over one shoulder. Now Ralph is a chonky boy and this took some doing, but I carried him outside and threw him across the backseat of the car. Then I went back in and grabbed Chloe.

Now, just to paint a picture for you, I was walking out of a strip club at one a.m., carrying an unconscious girl over my shoulder. If that doesn't look suspect, I don't know what does. As I exited the door there was a group of young guys clustered outside. They said nothing to me as I walked past with an unconscious chick slung over my shoulder. True heroes.

I threw her across the back seat on top of Ralph, who seemed to be regaining consciousness, and I began driving them back towards their apartment. At some point Ralph had managed to sit up. I tried communicating with him, but he was too drunk to speak English. He began making a retching sound, needing to puke. Luckily, I was prepared for such contingencies, and I handed him a grocery bag, which he held upside down.

"Ralph, turn it around."

He began retching.

"Inside the bag!" My preparation had been for naught. He puked on the wrong end of the bag, and it dribbled down onto his still unconscious wife, and more tragically, my car seats.

"Ralph!" I screamed. He began making more retching sounds. I rolled the rear window down for him.

"Out the window! Out the window!" To his credit, he did manage to get his head out of the window, but then he elected to puke into the wind, which blew much of it back into the car and onto his face, and on the inside of my back windshield. "God-damn it!" I screamed.

He burped, then smacked his lips.

"Savoring the taste?" I said.

He just cocked his head like a confused dog. Then his big dumb eyes locked onto his puke-covered wife. Through the review mirror, I saw the dumbest smile on his face. Then he began to stare at his wife's vomit-covered ass. He looked up at me through the rearview mirror.

"Dat ass!" he yelled.

I looked at him, feeling confused. What he did next would forever scar my memory, and I would forever associate this act with him. He took a flat palm, his eyes flashed between his flexed hand and Chloe's ass. We made eye contact in the mirror. He was grinning from ear to ear. "Dat ass!!" He said, then he began to spank Chloe's ass.

Smack! Slurp!

I looked back and saw him spanking his wife's vomit-covered ass, further spreading it around my car.

"Ralph! Stop that!"

"Dat asssss!"

Smack! Slurp!

"Bad! Bad! Ralph!" I said, trying to reach back and smack his hand away as I drove down a sketchy road at one o'clock in the morning.

"Dat aaaasssss!"

Smack! Slurp!

"Ralph! Quit slapping your wife's ass. You piece of shit!" He looked at me, his smile evaporated, and a jowly sad look came across his face. I guess I hurt his feelings. This was when he began to sob. I watched as his face turned red and he began crying, the ugly kind of crying, like how a four-year-old cries, with snot streaming down his face and all. I was at a loss for words. Then I heard my phone ring. I glanced and saw the caller ID: Pukestain.

"What does he want!" I said, knowing that this would probably spell even more trouble for me.

"What?" I answered impatiently.

"Dem gurls... day don't wuvv you... they just taka... ya money and leave," Pukestain said, quite remorsefully.

"No shit," I said.

"Ya man!" Pukestain said. I could hear the sound of traffic and a horn honk through the phone. "—Fuckkl you, man," Pukestain said to someone else.

"Pukestain, where the fuck are you?"

"I'mm walking back hommee, bunch a-holes out here honking at me,"

"Pukestain, where are you walking?" I asked and could hear honking and someone yelling at him.

"Downa roade, ebberrone is sucha a-hole..."

"Pukestain, get the fuck off the road. Go back to the strip club and I will come and get you." I said, knowing that I was already pretty far down the road.

"Okay... I wrillle waitt for you, but Imma not going back in with dem a-holes," he said, then hung up on me. I would later learn that he had been walking down the middle of the road, against traffic.

"Peee!" Ralph suddenly exclaimed. Turning my attention back to him, I saw he was grabbing his penis through his pants.

"You've got to pee?" I asked. He nodded his head furiously and began trying to wrench the door open. We were moving at fifty mph. He began to drunkenly fiddle with the lock. I knew that I had to pull over as quickly as possible.

I pulled into a sketchy gas station, and spotted a group of thuggish looking guys who were eyeballing us already. But before I could peel off and find an alternative location, Ralph had thrown open the door of the car and was stumbling into the darkness and into the ghetto neighborhood behind the gas sta-tion. Cursing my luck, I checked on Chloe to make sure she was still breathing, then exited the vehicle and locked the door. About ten gangsters stared at me. I ran into the darkness behind the gas station and didn't see Ralph.

"Ralph?" I said.

"Ahhhhhhh!" I heard, along with loud and very angry barking. I ran towards the sound, like those Marines in that stupid commercial where they jog towards danger. I found him, pants to his ankles—like a four-year-old at a urinal—peeing all too close to a pit bull through a chain-link fence.

"Ralph!" I gritted angrily.

Of course, he spun around, cock hanging out, still peeing. He finished, and I had to help him stumble back to the car. The thugs mean-mugged me, and I tried to look tough as I stuffed him in the back of my Civic.

We drove back without much further fanfare, because Ralph passed out again. We arrived at their apartment, and I tried to shake them both awake. They wouldn't budge, except to give me an annoyed moan. It was getting late, and I had formation early in the morning. I carried them up the stairs one by one and put them into bed. I set the alarm for him and informed him that we had PT at 0630.

But my night was not yet over. I went and recovered Pukestain, who was still quite distraught about the mean strippers. "C'mon, buddy. Let's get you home."

I barely made it on time to formation that morning, and needless to say, I never volunteered to DD for them again.

PEP IN MY STEP

This story occurred shortly after arriving at my Special Forces ODA.

I'd been banging hookers left and right, pretty much nonstop since my arrival. I learned through the grapevine that one of the girls I'd banged had just tested positive for HIV. Now I wasn't sure if it was just my imagination, but I began to feel a little ill, so I researched HIV symptoms, and tried to gauge what the odds were that I'd really gotten it. Apparently, for heterosexual men engaging in vaginal intercourse, the odds of contracting HIV are somewhere around 0.04%. Here's the thing though, as you can tell from some of my previous stories, I haven't always been the most careful. I'd been banging a lot of hookers. In my defense, they'd seemed trustworthy—but I did have a condom break on me. The more I thought about it, the more I realized that if I did have it, that I might've been a super spreader. I mean, I was getting around, as were the prostitutes. If I did have it, I could have many hookers' and johns' blood on my hands. Ethically, I felt I had to get tested.

I decided not to go the military route because this could carry with it a lot of unintended consequences. I would get flagged, and I could potentially get medically discharged without any benefits, since HIV contracted from a local hooker probably wouldn't be considered service connected. So I decided to find a discrete local clinic and pay out of pocket.

After a quick Google search, and some Google translating, I found a place that did HIV testing and could prescribe post-exposure prophylaxis (PEP). PEPs are taken after exposure to HIV and can prevent the virus from taking hold in the body, if taken within seventy-two hours. I hoped that if I had been exposed to it, I was still in this window.

I got a taxi and went over to the clinic.

In the clinic, I noticed there were a lot of local Filipino men and trannies. I was getting eyeballed. I tried to act natural and blend in, but surprise, there was no blending in.

I was called back to the examination room, and I struggled to communicate what I wanted through Google Translate. It seemed like they understood me, and they drew blood for what I hoped was HIV testing.

A staff member instructed me to wait out in the waiting room while they processed my results. Some chick with a dick sat next to me and tried chatting me up while I awaited my death sentence.

I was called back into the examining room, where a doctor who spoke very broken English told me that I was negative, I think. I hoped I wasn't just hearing what I wanted to. He did say that HIV can remain undetectable if I was still beneath the viral threshold. They handed me a bottle of pills. After translating, it seemed that I got what I'd come for—PEPs. I immediately started popping pills.

While undergoing this course of PEPs, I had to conduct live fire training exercises with the Filipino special forces. This wouldn't have been a problem, except for the fact that some of the side effects of the medications are vertigo and nausea. I had a decision to make. I could take the PEPs, and potentially prevent HIV from taking over my body, and conduct a live fire training exercise while feeling the earth spin around me, and potentially kill myself, a teammate, or a foreign national, straining US relations forever. Or I could not take the PEPs and cross my fingers and hope for the best on the HIV front.

I chose the latter.

Worst case scenario, I had HIV, and could just raw dog it all the time with the HIV gang; they were probably better in bed anyway.

After a couple of weeks and a blood test later, everything seemed good; I probably just had a cold or some other less serious virus. Honestly, the HIV scare shook me pretty bad. I beat myself up for being so sleazy. I mean, what had I come too? I had been raised better than this and came from a good family.

It was a fresh start in the life of Joe. I'd been gifted a new lease on life, and I would safeguard and protect this precious, wonderful life that I'd been given.

A week later, I found the madame in her usual spot, and the girls lined up, many of whom I'd already banged. But at the end of the lineup, I spotted a new girl. She was a bit shorter, plumper, with bigger tits. Fuck it.

I got her back to the hotel room, and then to the bedroom. She took off her booty shorts and underpants and stood before me with nothing but a t-shirt on. I laid on the bed waiting for more to be removed, and she crawled on top of me, but the shirt remained.

"Hey, can you take the shirt off?" I asked.

She shook her head in response. No? This was not cool. I picked her for her big titties and was hellbent on seeing them. Perhaps ten bucks would change her mind.

"Lose the shirt."

She lost the shirt, revealing nice tits, but a scar that ran from her lower abdomen down. I looked at the scar. She seemed self-conscious and said, "I lost my baby." This was a horribly bumming statement that didn't really put me in the mood, but between her and the hotel, I was already sixty bucks deep. I manned up and got right back at it.

As I was banging her in what is known as the "table top" position, I noticed that she clutched at the scar and began making a moaning sound, but not the sexy kind, the painful kind.

"What's wrong?" I asked.

"My scar hurts," she said. I stopped but she insisted on continuing. I kept banging her for a bit, but she kept moaning, which just wasn't doing it for me. At that point, I knew she wasn't going to make me cum.

I sighed, and pulled out of her, regretting being so sensitive to the needs of others, and instructed her to put her clothes back on. I checked my watch and realized that I might yet get a chance to blast a load into a Filipino because the madame was probably still running her product. All was not lost.

I hustled, called a taxi, and took the crying girl back down to the Madame. She looked at me, and back at the crying girl, and asked me, "Did she do good job?"

I shook my head. The madame began aggressively questioning the girl in Filipino. The girl cried and shook her head.

"I am sorry you no cum, mister, you want another girl?" she asked

"I would in fact," I said. The girls lined up in front of me, looking back between the crying girl and myself. They were probably a bit nervous and asking themselves what I did to her. But that would be sorted out as soon as they realized I was just a regular john.

At this point, I just wanted a sure-fire thing, someone dependable, so I picked a girl I'd banged before. Not the hottest, not even the best fucker, but someone who would get the job done.

I got a taxi. As me and ol' reliable drove away, I could hear the madame chastising the new girl. To me, this whole ordeal (though initially disappointing) was a stellar display of customer service. I returned the product, dissatisfied, and she replaced the product with a better product, without asking questions or trying to charge me more money—really stellar customer service. I can think of a few American companies that could learn a thing or two from the Filipino madame.

RANDOM TEXT MESSAGE FROM JOE

The following is a text exchange between me and Greg.

How's it's hanging bro? – Greg

T-16h Wake up with a hangover and a sore throat from crashing an open bar at a crossdressing dance performance.

T-12h Study for Harvard law school interview for an hour.

T-11h Slam a caffeine tablet and hit the gym for 3 hours while using and abusing Tinder, Bumble, and Okcupid.

T-7h Call the hooker I ordered. Y U late? Traffic b/c ash wed, fuck.

T-5h Hooker arrives with female pimp. I treat them to dinner. The fries are cold. Slam a beer and a Viagra.

T-4h Quality time.

T-3h Quality time part 2. Have to stop because I'm hitting her cervix. #smol.

T-2h Help the hooker negotiate with the pimp about the money split. She's only getting 1/3 of the pesos – wtf? Pimps are lyin' and cheatin'. I'll hook her up next time.

T-1h Escort hooker to pimp. Not my problem anymore. Buddy says come to the club.

Can't bro, I got an interview to ace.

T-30m Put on a white shirt and red tie (that's the school color). Read my resume again. Slam some preworkout with no water.

T-20m Vomit profusely. Preworkout is no joke.

T-10m Vomit again.

T-1m. Zoom is loading the chat. Vomit my brains out. Shirt looks legit tho.

T-0 Interview like a professional. Yahtzee.

T+30 Vomit 3 times in a row and shit my brains out. Always take preworkout with water.

T+1h Hound a YouTuber to shill my product line. Go to bed. Shit my pants. Slam an Imodium and go to bed again.
— Joe

Dots indicating that Greg is composing a response remain on the screen for a good five to ten minutes. Until finally:

Wow. That's wild bro — Greg

PART 3
MEDICAL MISHAPS

THE DICK BOMB

This story occurred while I was a Special Forces candidate. I was in holdover, waiting to begin the Q-course after selection, when I decided that I was going to get jacked. So I asked a guy named Ken, who I'd gone to basic training with, about roids. He'd always denied juicing, claimed to be natty, but I knew that there was no way this guy was able to recover from three workouts a day plus smoke sessions and PT and still be huge. Sure enough, over some beers, he admitted to "lightly using"; I pressed him for more details and asked for a point of contact. He obliged. He gave me the phone number of some guy, who in turn, gave me another guy's number. A chain of plausible deniability, I guess. I texted the guy.

"Hey Wayne, my name is Joe. This guy Ken gave me Rico's number who gave me your number. I'm looking for some product."

"What kind you want?"

"I don't know, just trying to get jacked."

"Alright, I'd recommend running some test and some TREN. I'll give you some stuff for a PCT afterward and a special bonus. Give you 10 weeks worth for $250."

"Sounds good. When and where can I pick up?" I texted.

I really had no idea what I was doing and decided to just trust the guy. I Googled some of the compounds he'd referred to and learned that Trenbolone is an anabolic agent originally designed to beef up meat cattle. Perfect, I thought. Before I knew it, I was driving to meet this random guy at a gas station towards Raleigh.

At the gas station, I spotted a shitty, dented Honda Element that matched the description the guy had given me. He was parked next to the vacuum station, far away from the pumps and the convenience store. I pulled my vehicle in behind his, making it look like I was waiting to use the vacuum myself. I got out of my vehicle and spotted a short, jacked dude in a hoodie.

"Hey, are you Wayne?" I said. The short, jacked dude with a thick beard looked at me with a sideways glance.

"You here for the gear?" he said. His lack of subtly worried me, but I still appreciated his rhyme. This was obviously a legit businessman.

"Yes."

He motioned for me to come over towards the passenger door facing away from the gas station. In the back he had a shoebox filled with a bunch of needles, vials, and pills. "Alright my dude, so this here is TREN." He picked up an unmarked vial with a brackish orange fluid inside of it. "You'll want to do about one milliliter twice a week. It should be about 250 milligrams a milliliter... And FYI, these have a little bit of a bite to them..."

"What do you mean bite?"

"They sting a bit, but you'll get used to it," Wayne said, which instantly assuaged my nerves. Wayne was jacked. I had nothing to fear. Wayne picked up another unmarked vial, this one with a much clearer fluid inside.

"This here is your test; again, you're gonna want to shoot this up twice a week, one milliliter. It should be about 250 milligrams per milliliter." Wayne put the vials back and pulled out a bag full of little white pills. "These are your PCT, the big ones are Clomid, and the small ones are Nolvadex. Two weeks after your last injection, you're gonna want to start off by taking two of each per day for one week. Then take one of each per day until you are out of pills. This should get your testicles back up and running." Wayne put the bag back into the shoe box.

Get my testicles back up and running? Maybe I hadn't thought this through completely. I had to decide quickly.

"Are these all coming from a pharmacy? What's your source?" I asked, feeling like a very savvy consumer for having asked such a question.

Wayne shook his head. "The pills are prescribed—pulled them from my personal prescription. The others though, I cooked up myself." Wayne said.

"Oh… are you like a chemist or something?" I asked, stupidly.

"No, I just watch a lot of YouTube and read a lot of Reddit. Ordered the raw chemicals from China and mixed them in my garage," Wayne said nonchalantly, giving me a slight shrug of his shoulders as if to say it was no big deal.

"And this is what you use?"

"Oh yeah," Wayne said. If it's good enough for Wayne, it's good enough for Joe. Wayne reached back into the shoe box and procured a Ziplock bag full of giant red and white-looking horse pills. A big smile came across Wayne's face.

"You're gonna love these, my dude. These here are a special concoction of my own design. They each contain 100mg of Viagra, 100mg of Cialis, and 300mg of caffeine. You will fuck like a machine and get a sick pump. I call them Dick Bombs." Wayne chuckled. He handed me the bag, which to me glowed like the Ark of the Covenant. I beheld these wonders of medical engineering, and in an instant, all of my doubts and concerns about Wayne's products dissipated.

"Wayne, you deserve a Nobel prize," I said.

"Hahaha, yeah, you're gonna love 'em, bro. Anyways my dude, good meeting you. If you need anything from me, feel free to hit me up," Wayne said, handing me the box. After giving him my payment, he gave me a vigorous shake with his meaty hand and sped off in his piece-of-shit Honda. I drove home, feeling like a new era had begun in the life of Joe, already daydreaming about the jacked sex god that I would become.

Upon return to the barracks, I found a place to stash the roids, where I figured the SF cadre would never look. I quickly got on Google and began to research how to properly cycle the compounds I had been given. Luckily the internet is chock full of forums, where various individuals discuss their cycles and how they went. Interestingly, in many of these forums, along with the username and comment, they also list body measurements along with a picture of the commentator. I sifted through lots of advice with no idea how to discern good from bad, until I decided that I would simply listen to the guys with the biggest bicep measurements. From my "research" I determined that Wayne's prescribed cycle wasn't particularly crazy or anything.

The next night I decided it was time to do it. I pulled up a YouTube video of a guy demoing how to inject steroids into the quadriceps. I chose the quadriceps because it seemed like it would be easier to put the needle in the right place, and it wouldn't require awkwardly twisting around, as it would if I were to inject into my ass.

Feeling very nervous, I set about sterilizing the injection site, and loading up a syringe. I'd read that you could inject as much as two milliliters in any one injection, and that you could load both compounds into a single syringe. So I took the needle, inserted it into the vial of testosterone, and very slowly and painfully drew up the fluid with the 26-gauge needle. This took forever, and I wondered if I was doing it wrong, until at long last it hit the one milliliter mark. I then took the same needle stuck it into the bottle of TREN, and drew the rusty liquid into the syringe. This fluid was thick and flowed more slowly.

Finally, I had two milliliters loaded up with steroids. I cleared the syringe of excess air as I learned from YouTube. Then I rewatched the video to ensure that I was targeting the correct portion of my quad. I positioned the 1.5-inch needle above the spot, like the killer in a slasher film, at a ninety-degree angle. I took a deep inhale. Sweat had beaded on my forehead as I pushed the needle towards my leg. The needle shook in the air; my hand trembled like I was having a fucking seizure. I felt like I suddenly had cerebral palsy. My head was feeling light. *Maybe I should back out of this before something bad happens,* I thought. *Don't be a fucking bitch,* another part of me responded. And I shakily drove that needle into my leg.

At first the skin indented; the needle didn't puncture. It turns out I had probably dulled it after inserting it into two different vials. I pushed a bit harder and punctured the skin, driving it fully into my quad. Nausea hit me immediately, and I thought I might pass out. Then my quad spasmed, like I had hit a nerve or something, but there was no blood or anything. I depressed the plunger and felt the two milliliters of fluid slowly pump into my quadriceps. It was a warm sensation at first, followed by a mild burning feeling. Wayne did say it would have a bit of "bite." Despite this, I fully depressed the plunger and pumped it all in, then shakily withdrew the needle. I did it quickly because I feared snapping off the needle beneath the skin, which would've made a very awkward trip to the ER. After disposing the needle, I sat back and tried to catch my breath. I felt sweaty and ill but was relieved to have survived the experience. And it would all be worth it. I would look back and laugh at this after I'd become a jacked sex god.

♦

The next day, I awoke, and felt a sharp pain in my quad where I injected. I looked at the site and saw that it had grown red and inflamed. I stood up out of my bed and instantly my right leg buckled. A hot pain radiated up and down my quad emanating from the injection site. *Fuck fuck fuck,* I thought. I hobbled over to the bathroom to get a better look at it. I for sure had a knot in my quad and it hurt like a motherfucker. I did some Googling, and it seemed unlikely that an infection could've taken hold this fast, which was my chief concern. It was six in the morning when I began to text and call Wayne repeatedly.

"Helllooooo?"

"Wayne, its Joe, from yesterday. I injected some into my quad, and now I've got a huge knot in my quad that's a bit red, and I can't fucking walk," I said.

"Oh yeah, bro, like I said, it's got a bit of bite to it," Wayne said.

"A bit of bite? This shit hurts real bad, dude," I said.

"Yeah, well, the quad is sensitive, and your body just needs to get used to it."

"You're sure it's not an infection or something?"

"Nah, just give it a couple of days, bro, and inject it into your ass next time. Later, dude." Wayne hung up on me.

"Fuck." I thought that Wayne seemed pretty confident. Then I remembered that Wayne is jacked, and I hoped that I hadn't just sounded like a little bitch. So I decided not to worry about it. I'd keep an eye on it and just tough it out for a few days.

I hobbled for about a week. I told everyone that I'd just twisted my ankle, which miraculously got me out of some PT. I carried on injecting the vile mixture, trying various other spots after attempting my ass, which I found caused both of my ass cheeks to hurt so bad that I couldn't sit comfortably. After this I attempted my shoulders, which had the unfortunate side effect of rendering me unable to lift my arm. *I'll get used to it,* I thought.

It turns out that Wayne was full of shit. After several weeks, I wasn't getting used to it all. I was just in pain, sweaty, and murderously horny. Let me tell you, if I wasn't engaged in cadre organized bullshit, I was swiping right on Tinder like it was my full-time job.

I was on a date with this blonde bimbo in Raleigh. It seemed to be going pretty well. We'd just finished dinner and we were about to head back to her place. I snuck off into the bathroom and fished inside of my pocket until I grasped one of the Dick Bombs that Wayne had given me. The huge red and white homemade pill shone with the promise of a wild night. I downed it, then returned to my date and began to drive us back to her place.

On the drive back she pats my thigh, a promising sign. Fifteen minutes into the drive, I begin to get a head rush—must be the caffeine. Shortly thereafter, I began to feel a little congested, like my nose was constricting. Then I developed a pounding headache and a rock-hard erection, and my heart began to pound. I thought I might be about to have a heart attack, but I played cool, not wanting to ruin my chances with bimbo.

We arrived at her place and she invited me inside. She pulled me into a bedroom that did not have a bed. We made out. We were on the floor, my pants were down, but underwear was on, and she was in the same configuration. She was straddling on top of me, grinding her panty-covered pussy against my dick, and making out with me like her life depended on it.

Things seemed to be going well. I felt like my cock was about to tear through my underwear and through her panties, so I began to remove them. She stopped me.

"Not on a first date buddy," she said, then continued to make out with me. My headache had not dissipated, and my cock was so hard I worried that I was going to rupture a vein—I hoped she was at least impressed by it. I tried not to think about it or panic, and proceeded to make out with her for quite some time.

She didn't want me to go, and in fact I'm quite sure she would've made out with me all night, but I'm not in high school. I was pretty certain that if I didn't cum soon, that my dick might actually explode. I went back to my barracks and rubbed one out.

Once I was done, my dick was still hard. I laid on my side with my dick erect and rigid like a fucking kickstand all night.

The next morning, I woke up with the most epic morning wood of my life. I see that I have a text on my phone.

"You should head on over and have breakfast at my place. I look forward to our second date ;)" the bimbo texted me.

"I'll head on over," I responded.

I grabbed an overnight bag and reached for the Dick Bombs in my drawer. I studied the red and white pill, and wondered whether it would be wise to consume another one. This chick was going to be voracious—I knew that I would get laid. She was like a high-school-girl-at-prom kind of horny. Wisely, I knocked back another pill and washed it down with a full bottle of Gatorade. I now had somewhere around 200mg of Viagra, 200mg of Cialis, and somewhere between 350 to 600mg of caffeine pumping through my veins. Oh, and of course the Trenbolone.

Turns out, the bitch was a liar. There was no breakfast; I got mauled by a girl in lingerie as soon as I crossed the threshold. I carried her to the room, ripped off her panties, which were already wet, condomed up, and thrust into her. My head was throbbing. I could feel my heart beat in my eyes, face, and cock, which literally jumped with each pulsation. I was full of energy and still horny from last night. We started hard. She was squirting all over me, making a fucking mess of the bed. She came, I came. She was delighted to see I was still hard and began blowing me, though she really didn't need to, then slid me inside her again.

My cock was so hard that it was tearing through condoms. She orgasmed as my high velocity nut smacked into her uterus. She was loving it and fucking insatiable. Five times in a row we went, without stopping, and I was still hard.

I could no longer tell if my cock was hurting from the rough sex or from the copious amounts of drugs pumping through my system. Either way, I felt fairly certain that I was facing a medical emergency and needed to do something about it. I did notice that the pain seemed to abate after I came, so I decided that I just needed to keep cumming.

She had gone to the kitchen to rehydrate. I came up behind her and grabbed her by the hair, she hurriedly hiked down her pants, and I bent her over and fucked her again.

Pussy juice and cum dribbled onto the floor, and I was beginning to lose my footing. We fucked again on the table, then the couch, the bed two more times, she stopped to take some Motrin, then we did it some more, standing, laying, kneeling, acrobatic fucking. I was giving her everything I had, and she was enduring it, somehow. She was an insatiable sex fiend. I had to slay her.

We'd quiver, cum, and collapse, only for her to crawl towards me like some heroin addict saying "again." Again, we'd got to the point where it became just as much about defeating her as it was about relieving my never-ending erection.

When all was said and done, we fucked well north of twenty times in a twenty-four-hour period. She laid on her side in ecstatic pain, clutching her abdomen and icing her pussy. I had conquered her. I'd slain my Grendel.

Unfortunately, she was decommissioned for a little over a week, bleeding and sore as shit, and her stomach hurt. The poor girl had to call in sick from work for the week. The rest of our short time together was quite lame.

I'd survived the experience, even though I'd overdosed on Dick

Bomb. I did have a pretty wicked nose bleed that lasted a couple of days, and my body was still fucking hurting from all the bullshit juice Wayne had given me.

Even with all that, I felt like an absolute stud, and pitied whatever poor fucking sap dated her next.

DIRTY DANCING

This story occurred while at my unit in the 82nd.

It was a Friday night at the barracks and we were planning on throwing a real rager in my room. We had string lights, a fog machine, bumping music, a disco ball, repelling ropes, fluid IVs, smelling salts, tourniquets, Coors, Military Special vodka—the whole shebang. These parties were usually sausage fests. though sometimes there were civilian women who would turn up to these parties. As previously described, these women are colloquially referred to as "barracks bunnies." Anyhow… none of that concerned me, as I was in a committed long-term relationship.

Throwing barracks ragers allowed me to hang with the boys and watch the shit show. My room on the third floor was the place to be. High enough and far enough inside that MPs wouldn't bother us. After all, we didn't ID people at the door. You know, typical barracks room shit with a bunch of guys, getting wild and getting into fights. Pretty much everyone understood that as long as we could contain our guys and not let them outside of the barracks compound, we could handle any issues that might arise internally. Surprise, surprise, issues always arose.

When you mix eighteen to twenty-four-year-olds in the same barracks, underage drinking is bound to happen. It's supposed to happen, like the college experience for guys who couldn't get into college.

It was getting into the funky hours. Everyone had been off duty since around two p.m. We'd received our safety briefing, you

know the typical:
"Don't drink and drive."
"Don't beat your spouse."
"Don't butt chug ethanol."
"Don't buy a Camaro with 29% APR."
"Don't rape anybody."
"Don't get into a fight at the bar… but if you do, win."
"Don't repel off the side of the barracks."
Etc.

Now it was nine p.m. and everyone had been drinking since two p.m. Guys were walking around the barracks drunk as shit. Guys started piling into my room for the party. There were a few chicks in there, and a guy was dancing with them. More guys danced in around them, hoping to steal them away, like birds-of-paradise engaging in their courtship dance. The barracks bunnies would disappear off somewhere with a guy, only to return twenty minutes later.

The party raged on, and this older guy showed up, a crusty staff sergeant who'd recently been consigned to the barracks after an ugly divorce. He showed up at the party very drunk and ready to mingle and immediately went onto the "dance floor" of my barracks room. Now I stood by with my friend, Greg, and watched in horror as this man whipped out a knife with a large fixed blade, like a Rambo knife. Before anything could be done, he made a clapping motion. He stabbed his palm, pierced right through it, like Jesus being nailed down. He ripped it back out, and continued dancing, like nothing had happened.

After overcoming both surprise and momentary confusion, Greg sprang into action, tackling him into the nearby bathroom and wresting the Rambo knife from him. With the dangerous part out of the way, I came in to assist Greg.

"Hey, Greg, get his hand into the bathtub. He's bleeding all over my shit," I directed. Greg, being a total bro, complied.

"We should probably get a tourniquet on this guy," Greg gritted.

"Yeah, that's probably a good idea," I said, as blood spurted onto the walls of the shower-tub. Hurriedly, I grabbed my IFAC, a soldier medical kit attached to my body armor in a nearby closet. I gathered up a pressure bandage and a tourniquet, then Greg and I got to work. First, we applied the tourniquet high and tight, then wrapped his hand with a pressure bandage. We quickly got the bleeding under control. By this point, quite a commotion had begun. One of the barracks bunnies had slipped on the blood and led a mass exodus out of the barracks. Like the pied piper, she led the horny partiers out of my barracks room, leaving it pretty empty.

"Hey man, you good?" I asked the divorcee.

"Errrggggehhh," he uttered.

"What's your name?" Greg asked.

"Ergggghhhhhh," the casualty responded.

"This guy is beyond fucking hammered," Greg said.

"Yeah, no shit, what the hell are we supposed to do with him?"

"Uhgu,rggugugoguhhhhhhh," the casualty said.

"I've already called 911," said a guy behind us. My eyes about bugged out of my head when he said this. This guy was drunk as fuck, at a barracks party in my room that involved a lot of underaged drinking. There was no fucking way I would be getting out of this scot-free; who was gonna believe that this guy just stabbed himself in the hand? Especially with the room looking like a goddamned crime scene. Besides that, I'd definitely gotten my DNA all over the guy. God forbid this dude fucking died. I might get charged with murder. *Fuck!*

"Alright, we need to think.... Greg, help me *think*!" I said.

Greg's eyes were wide as he looked around frantically. "We should probably clean this up!" he said.

"Yeah, no shit, what the fuck do we do with this fucking idiot?" I said, nodding towards the guy we had pinned down.

"Uhhh... let's get him off the X?" Greg asked.

Like that, a light bulb lit up above my head, like I'd been struck by holy lightning and divine wisdom. "Alright, let's get him downstairs and beat the MPs. We can say we just found him like this."

Greg locked eyes with me, staring in disbelief. "You think that'll work?" he asked.

"Do you have a better idea?"

"Nope," he said.

"Then it's settled."

Hurriedly we mopped up the floor, cleaning up the crime scene as best as we could, while our casualty lay in the corner in the fetal position. We tried to be as quick and thorough as we could while racing against the clock.

One of our buddies agreed to continue cleaning while Greg and I extracted the casualty out of my room. I got under one of his shoulders and Greg got under the other, and we slowly moved the drunk, tourniqueted man with bloody gauze down the stairs and onto the grassy knoll next to the parking lot, as inconspicuously as we could. As we got down to the ground floor, the ambulance pulled up.

The paramedic saw him. "Sir, are you alright?" he asked our wounded fellow who responded, "hurrrhhuuu?" The paramedic looked at him quizzically then back to me and Greg.

"We think he's pretty drunk," I said to him.

The paramedic nodded his head. "How did this happen?" he asked.

"We just found him out here like this. No clue, but he had stabbed himself with this," I said, and handed the paramedic the knife. The paramedic's eyebrow pricked up, and he looked between Greg and me. I felt my pulse quicken. *Did I just fuck myself?*

"Well, thank God you guys found him. He might've bled out," he said.

"Not all heroes wear capes," Greg said, and both the paramedic and I looked at him disapprovingly.

Much to our surprise and relief, there weren't a lot of follow-up questions. The paramedics took him off our hands, and the lout was too drunk to remember what had happened.

But who carries that big of a knife to a mass event? Well, this wasn't exactly a mass event, but the question remains, why? I never did see him again after that incident, and nothing came of it.

BURSTING MY BURSA

I'd just graduated basic combat training (BCT) and was in Airborne holdover. For many, this was the end of the road. They'd completed BCT and were shipped off to their new units. We were all so convinced that we'd one day see each other again. For the most part, we never did.

Though many had left, still many remained, including those of us destined for Airborne School, Special Forces Assessment and Selection, or Ranger Assessment and Selection. I'm sure this sounds cool and all, but what it really meant was that we would remain in TRADOC (Army Training Command), and continue to be treated like basic trainees for the foreseeable future.

After the celebrations were over, those of us remaining in TRADOC boarded a bus to head over to our next thing. We packed into the bus with our duffel bags like cattle, as we'd been doing for the past sixteen weeks. We moved down the street to an equally unfriendly environment: "Airborne Holdover."

Once again, we were assigned bunk beds in an open floor area. We still conducted regular PT, attended accountability formations every couple of hours, and still had to march to the chow hall in formation—very little had changed. I took solace in the fact we were only going to stay here for a week, and after that we'd move on to Airborne School. But things didn't go according to plan.

During a light-hearted barracks brawl, I scuffed up my elbow. I washed the little red gash and didn't worry about it until a couple of days later when it started to throb. Since we weren't allowed to have any medications (i.e. I couldn't have Neosporin), nor was I allowed to shop for anything, I wound up reporting in to sick call.

"It's just a boo boo… You're fine," said the Army medic, turning me away.

"Can you give me some Neosporin so it doesn't get infected?" I said.

"No… go away," he said. I shook my head and walked off, frustrated. I was used to lackluster treatment from sick call, and this was the same sick call that had failed to treat a MRSA infection that I'd incurred during basic, an infection that had landed me in the hospital.

It was no secret that the medics at the Fort Benning facility were not particularly attentive. They tended to assume that anyone reporting to sick call was nothing more than a lazy private trying to get out of morning PT. Unfortunately, due to rules and unhelpful cadre, they were my only option. Since I was still under TRADOC, I could not leave the base or make any appointments for myself.

The infection grew worse over the next couple of days. I showed up to sick call three days in a row until I developed a massive subcutaneous cyst that had inflated like a balloon up my forearm.

They took me to a room in the back filled with basic trainees on exam tables. A medic assigned me a table. A basic trainee to my left screamed as a nurse stabbed and squeezed a giant cyst on his foot. I watched him, knowing that I was next; he was just being dramatic—I hoped.

The medic sat on a stool next to me and instructed me to straighten my arm out across a table he wheeled up between us. He poked at the bulging cyst in my forearm. "Specialist, why didn't you report to sick call sooner?" he said condescendingly.

"Sergeant, I've been here four times in the last week trying to prevent this from happening, but ya'll kept turning me away," I said.

"Don't get sassy with me, Specialist," he said. I wondered if he remembered turning me away. "We're gonna need to drain this thing," he said. "Turn your arm over." I attempted to turn my arm 180 degrees but found that I couldn't get into the position he desired—strangely.

He roughly began to inspect the injury site, a bright red cut right on the elbow. He procured a foot-long wooden Q-tip from a nearby jar. With one hand he pushed down behind my elbow, pinning my arm down, and with the other he guided the wooden Q-tip into the meaty cut, and up into the wound channel. It hurt pretty bad, but I refused to give him the satisfaction of a moan. I watched as the outline of the Q-tip under my skin moved up into the giant cyst.

"Hold still, I've got to pop the infection sack," he said. The medic then drew the Q-tip back like he was shooting billiards, and then rammed it forward into the hard edge of the 'infection sack'—repeatedly. The infection sack was surprisingly durable, and it required repeated ramming. I clenched my teeth as he smashed into the sensitive infected tissue inside my arm. The rough Q-tip felt like it was sawing at my skin from the inside.

Eventually, he penetrated the infection sack, and the tip of the stick pierced the tender cyst. It popped, and pus ran down the channel and out through the wound; the big cyst slowly deflated. With pus streaming out, the medic began to draw the Q-tip back out of the elbow. It was 9/10ths of the way out when it snagged on something. Without hesitation, the medic put both hands on the wooden Q-tip and pulled at it like a lawn mower's rip cord. It came free, puss and blood flew into the air, and a wiggly chunk of meat fell from the Q-tip onto the medical tray. We both stared at the curious, sack-like, bloody membrane that lay on the table. The medic scratched his head. A curious physician's assistant ambled over.

"It must be the edge of his infection sack," the medic said. He looked up at the physician's assistant nervously.

She shook her head. "No, I think you just removed a piece of his bursa," she said. I was too busy basking in the euphoria one gets after being in excruciating pain to care too terribly.

"Insert some gauze, and let's wrap up his arm. He's going to need to be on profile for a while," she said.

Hearing this refocused my attention. "Wait… profile? How long? I'm shipping off to Airborne School next week!" I said.

She shook her head. "No, you won't. You need to heal, and we need to get this infection under control. You will keep this arm wrapped and immobilized." she said. The shooting pain in my elbow seemed to confirm her assessment. She explained to me the function of a bursa, which is, apparently, pretty critical to healthy joint function; and also, that infection was still a major concern.

This was a pretty bad experience with Army medical. But alas, it would not be my last. If you think this is bad, you should brace yourself for what happens in the next section.

PART 4
THE DERRIERE DIARY

PREFACE TO THE DERRIERE DIARY

In this section I will recount a story in multiple parts; this may be the most outlandish, wildest, most disturbing and preposterous thing you've ever heard or read.

MY THIRD BUTT CHEEK: PART ONE

This story occurred while in special operations. It had only been a few weeks since I arrived in Ethiopia, and already I'd overcome both culture shock and a vicious stint of diarrhea.

Already in my nascent deployment, a new challenge emerged: pain in my ass. It wasn't colon or sphincter related; instead, I felt a sharp pain between my asshole and the base of my tailbone.

First, I fingered around the area, seeing if a tick or some other insect had found its way into my ass crack, but I found nothing, so I carried on like I normally did. But as the pain persisted I began to get concerned. I bent over and spread my cheeks, as you do, and tried to get a look at the source in the dingy mirror. As it turns out, trying to examine one's ass crack while upside down and staring at a mirror from between your own legs is quite challenging. I grabbed my phone, spread my cheeks as best as I could with just one hand, and tried taking selfies of the area with the other.

I straightened upright and let the blood flow out of my head for a second. I flipped through the pictures; mostly they were just of the backside of my testicles and asshole. I bent over again, took some more pics and popped back up. Finally, I had a clear picture. There was my asshole, clear as day, then another small dark pit above my asshole. I rubbed at the area, thinking maybe it was just a piece of debris, and took another picture. I confirmed there was a hole above my asshole. Naturally, I sent a picture of the pit, along with my asshole and the back of my testicles to my friend, who is a Special Forces medic. I wanted his feedback.

I then did a quick Google search of "hole above my asshole," and zeroed in on a likely candidate: pilonidal cyst.

According to WebMD, pilonidal is the amalgamation of Latin and Greek words: "pilus" (hair) and "nidal" (nest), or "hair nest," that refers to an ingrown hair that creates tunnels inside of you that form a nest-like structure that gets infected. Under treatment options it said surgery and antibiotics; I began to get nervous. If this was a pilonidal cyst, it was pretty terrible timing.

While I waited for my SF medic friend to respond, I went downstairs to see if I could find the Civil Affairs team medic who shared our team house with us.

"Medic? Medic?" I said. I knocked on a couple of doors until I found him.

The medic emerged with glassy eyes, and I assumed that he'd been smoking pot again. I informed him of the situation and told him that I had something for him to look at. We went back into his room. I dropped drawers, and—in a dignified manner—bent over and spread my butt cheeks.

He looked at it and concurred that it must be a pilonidal cyst. He suggested cutting into it right then and there, but I declined the offer. I thought I would let him reevaluate me when he wasn't high. I touched base with Craig and Dufus (my NCOIC and OIC respectively) and told them what I'd just found. They told me to go to the embassy doctor.

At the embassy, Dr. Odinga, a gentle older man with thick spectacles and an even thicker Ethiopian accent, saw me. I spread my cheeks for him. He looked at it, scratched his head, then proceeded to disappear from the office, leaving me with my ass out.

A while later, he returned, smiling. "Mr. Joe, what you have I believe is a pilonidal cyst… the word pilonidal is the amalgamation of Latin and Greek words 'pilus' meaning hair and 'nidal' meaning nest or hair nest, that refers to an ingrown hair that creates tunnels inside of you that form a nest-like structure that gets infected," he said.

I nodded my head, pretty sure he had just gone and queried Google with: "hole above asshole." Oh boy. Should I be worried?

"Mr. Joe, if you could just bend forward and allow me to measure the hole," he said.

I obliged and spread my cheeks as much as I could for the guy. He took a Sharpie and drew a circle around my pilonidal cyst, then tape measured it.

"Mr. Joe, you can stand back up." As I stood and pulled my pants up, Dr. Odinga scribbled away on a notepad. Eventually, he finished his work, and then proceeded to turn it around and show it to me: it was a fairly rudimentary picture of my ass. He'd just painted me like one of his French girls, I thought. He put a finger on the drawing.

"This here is your butthole." He then traced his finger up to the next hole. "That is your pilonidal cyst," he said, in his thick African accent. *What would I do without you,* I thought. "Mr. Joe, this may resolve itself given some time. We will keep an eye on it, though, and see if it gets better or worse. Come back here in two weeks."

Two weeks later, there was even more pain in my ass. So I bent over and once again gave the cheeks the ol' spread, and discovered that I was now sporting another hole. I was now up to three holes (including my butthole, for those of you keeping a tally). I informed Craig and Captain Dufus of this, and Craig laughed. "So you have three assholes."

"Yes, thank you for the insight, Craig."

I went and showed the in-house medic, who did an examination and laughs like this was some little joke for him. He told me,

"Yeah man, it kinda looks like you have three buttholes now." Did I ever mention to you how much I valued his medical wisdom?

I went back to Dr. Odinga, who was very fascinated by all of this. "Yes, yes, it is getting bigger; looks like it has made multiple holes."

"Thank you, doctor."

"I want you to go to Jabali Hospital and get an ultrasound of the wound so we can see what it looks like on the inside."

I navigated my way through a weird tent-filled hospital only to find out that the African hospital has surprisingly never heard of Tricare, the insurance provider of the military. I called Tricare and explained to them the situation, and they promptly found a way to pay the hospital.

With payment sorted out, I hung out in the waiting room, until a large African woman in scrubs that were many sizes too small came and got me. We walked down a tight and dimly lit hospital corridor, until she pointed me to a room, then onto a bed, where I assumed the position: pants down and ass out. The nurse wasted no time (and provided no warning) before lathering a handful of cold petroleum jelly right on my cyst and asshole. She then got to work, passing the ultrasound against my holes and then gathering up the results.

"Mr. Joe, we will email you the results. You may pull your pants up," she said, and handed me a wad of paper towels to wipe off the lube. I slid my drawers up and felt petroleum gel slide down my ass. I guess I was in a hurry to get out of there and didn't really take the time to get it all off. I left the hospital feeling a bit defiled, but eager to receive my results.

I received the email of the ultrasound, which came in as a couple of JPEGS. I opened them up and quickly realized that I had no idea what I was looking at. I emailed the photos to Dr. Odinga and the Tricare medical team.

When I visited Dr. Odinga's office, he informed me that the cyst was still pretty shallow and would entail a minor excision. My medic looked it over and concurred with the conclusion. I also touched base with the Tricare overseas team, who reviewed it and thought it would require a very minor procedure as well.

Dr. Odinga referred me to a surgeon to get an opinion on what we should do about it. Craig and Dufus thought this was a good idea and told me to go to Jabali. I also discussed the issue with Tricare representatives and they informed me that Jabali was a network-approved hospital and would be a fine place to receive such a minor procedure.

I walked into Jabali Hospital with my approval from Tricare and went up into their general surgical suite. It was a fairly rundown, spiraling building with rooms connected via an outside banister, much like a motel. I walked into the surgical office and was immediately hit with the scent of incense and curry. Behind the front desk was an older lady in traditional Indian regalia.

"Hello," I said. "I'm looking to schedule a surgical consultation."

She looked up at me and responded, "Okay, if you can just have a seat, Doctor Kapoor will be out to see you shortly."

"Oh, you mean right now… great." I sat down, surprised that I could walk in and get seen by a surgeon immediately.

A few moments later, from a door behind the front desk emerged a small, elderly man with thin wispy hair that revealed the liver spots on his scalp. He was at least a foot shorter than me and had a bit of a limp. He smiled at me.

"Hello, I'm Doctor Kapoor. Please come into my office." I shook his tiny hand and followed him back into his office.

The office was small and had a wooden desk decorated with traditional Hindu religious items. Behind the desk was a bookshelf full of medical textbooks, and across from the desk on the opposite wall was an examination table. It was a modest room that reflected the gentle, intellectual nature of its occupant.

"So tell me, what brings you in today?" asked Dr. Kapoor.

"Dr. Kapoor, I work over at the US embassy, and the doctor there, along with my insurance provider, referred me over here so you could check out this issue I've been having…" I struggled for words to politely describe my problem.

"You see, I seem to have formed some holes over my tailbone, and the embassy doctor thinks I have a pilonidal cyst," I said to him. One of his bushy eyebrows perked. "That's what my team medic says, and the embassy doctor. They wanted you to take a look at it, to give me advice as to what to do with it," I said, waiting for him to respond.

"Okay, why don't you pull your pants down and get on the table and show me." I obliged him and got on the table, spreading my cheeks for yet another person. To my surprise, he didn't even wear gloves as he examined me, and was not shy at all about grabbing my cheeks and spreading them even further apart while he moved his face fairly close to my asshole. After examining my ass, he instructed me to get up and take a seat at his desk. He sat on the other side and got onto his computer to look something up.

"Ah yes, you have a pilonidal cyst," he said, confirming what I already knew. "Pilonidal is the amalgamation of a Latin and Greek words: 'pilus' (hair) and 'nidal' (nest), or 'hairnest,' that refers to an ingrown hair that creates tunnels inside of you that form a nest-like structure that gets infected," he said. I was beginning to wonder whether these people actually went to medical school or simply relied on doctor Google to get them through their day.

"Yes, yes, it is infected. You are going to require surgery. Have you had any imaging done of it?" he asked.

"Yes, I can send it to you right now," I said. I quickly got onto my phone and forwarded him the email with the images. After some time, he received them and gave them a look over.

"Yes, yes, it is indeed infected, but it doesn't look like the hair has burrowed down very far. Which is good. This means we caught it early! We can schedule the surgery very soon and get you back to normal again." He smiled at me whimsically.

I had a few questions for him though. "So what will the procedure look like?"

"I will make a small incision, remove the cyst and necrotic tissue, then sew it up."

"I like lifting weights and working out. How long will it be before I can return to those activities?"

"Four weeks, and you'll be fully healed and back to normal activities," he said, which was good news to me. It sounded like this was going to be a relatively minor procedure.

"Okay, can you write me a note of everything you want to do? So I can pass it along to my teammates, command, and insurance company and run it by them first."

"Absolutely." He proceeded to jot some things down by hand. I thanked him for his time, left the hospital, and found a driver to take me back to the team house.

Later, I presented the note to Creepy Craig, Dufus, the medic, the embassy doctor, as well as the Tricare medical team. Under the advisement of my team leader, detachment sergeant, CA team medic, Tricare medical team, and the embassy doctor, a surgery was scheduled. The Tricare medical team, medic, and embassy doctor all vouched for the surgeon and told me that Jabali was a vetted and approved hospital. My team leader and NCOIC told me that the rear was aware of the situation, and I was good to go.

MY THIRD BUTT CHEEK: PART TWO

The day of the surgery arrived; I went to the hospital with the CA team medic. We checked in at the counter and waited in the common area for a while. In a previous consultation with Dr. Kapoor, he'd agreed to let the CA medic come with him into the back room to supervise the surgery.

They brought me to my hospital room, where I stashed my overnight bag, donned my hospital gown, and sat on the bed eagerly awaiting my next task. The medic observed as the nurse drew my blood. The nurse, a surly woman, did not use a vacutainer, which is one of those fancy twentieth century blood-drawing instruments that you can simply attach the vials to. She instead took a very large needle, stuck it directly into the vein, and pulled it back. She missed the vein—a bunch of times—and fished the syringe beneath the skin again searching for it. I was looking at the medic nervously; he seemed interested but unperturbed by it all. She eventually got some blood into the sy-ringe but then faced her next challenge of getting it into the vial. She tried puncturing the rubber seal on the vial to squirt the blood from the syringe into it, but she found that this was taking longer than she would've liked it to.

Instead, she unscrewed the sterile lids off the top of the vials, removed the needle from the syringe, and proceeded to shoot the blood—quite forcefully—from the syringe into the various vials.

She did this directly over my hospital gown and got blood all over me. She'd evidently put too much blood into one of the vials and not the other, so like a mad scientist, she poured the blood from one vial into the other. All the while she was spilling more blood over me.

After this horrifying display of medical professionalism, I turned to the medic and said, "Hey E, I'm getting a really bad feeling about this place, man."

He waved his hand dismissively. "Don't worry about it, man, I'm sure you'll be fine."

I decided that I was just letting my nerves get the best of me, and decided to entrust the special operations medic, Tricare medical team, embassy doctor, and my leaders.

Next, a team of Ethiopian nurses arrived with a bed on wheels and instructed me to hop on, which I did. With the medic in tow, I was wheeled down into the pre-operations room.

I lay on my back in the preparations room with the medic next to me. The medic had a hairnet and gear on, all ready to come into the back with me when the time came. The anesthesiologist came by and introduced himself as Doctor something. He was a smiley, professorial-looking Ethiopian man. The medic liked him.

Next, the man of the hour arrived. Dr. Kapoor. He came in wearing dress shoes, beige slacks, scrubs and a surgical cap already. He explained that the surgical suite was still in use, so we would have to wait a while longer before we could proceed.

(2 hours later)

Finally, the previous surgery had wrapped up, and the room had been sanitized, I think. There was one slight curveball. At the last second, the hospital ward decided that the medic would not be allowed in the operating room. This panicked me at first, and I considered aborting, but the medic reminded me that it was a very small procedure and he'd be just outside the room. I decided that I was just being a pussy and letting my nerves get the best of me.

The nurses wheeled me to the operating room. The double doors swung open as they pushed me feet first into the room. The ceiling was high, and the room was large. Around twenty Ethiopian staff—some in scrubs—ambled about the room in its dim recesses near the walls and desks. At the center of the room was a stainless steel operating table that shone brightly from the pendant light that hung directly above. From a corner of the room, where many Ethiopians were gathered, a radio played some seventies or eighties music. I did not recognize the song, but it had a porny quality to it; the lyrics went: "oooooooh yahhhhhh babbbbbbayyyyy…"

I wasn't sure if I was about to have a surgery performed or get gang banged by a bunch of Ethiopians. The nurse parked my bed parallel to the operating table, which I noticed was a stark cold thing without pads nor face cutout. It reminded me of an autopsy table. The nurse hit the hydraulics on my bed, trying to raise it as high as she could, but it got stuck about a foot short of being even with the operating table. The flummoxed nurse consulted with some other Ethiopians, who took turns examining the hydraulics of my bed. They kept looking from me to the table, and I could tell they were trying to figure out how they were going to lift the 265-pound Mzungu. I offered to get on the operating table for them, but they declined.

I looked to my left where I spotted the surgeon, sitting on a short stool near the radio. He was scrubbed up, staring blankly at the floor, and seemed to be mouthing the lyrics. I smiled and tried to make eye contact with him, but he did not notice me. I figured that this was his pre-operation ritual, like Tom Brady mentally preparing himself before taking the field. I decided I didn't want to disrupt that.

Suddenly, from my left, a Ethiopian came flying towards me on a wheelie chair like a kid racing around an office building. The back of the chair faced me and just before he would've careened into me, the anesthesiologist spun to face me, and planted his feet on the ground to stop. He came to a stop perfectly beside my bed. "Hello," he said in an extra thick Ethiopian accent.

"It is da time to give you da medicine, please hold out ya arm," he said. I saw that he was quite skilled with a wheelie chair and was wearing a white lab coat, so I proffered him my arm.

He stabbed me with a needle, then pushed something into my veins. "You should be feelin' like you had one or maybe two Tuskers," he said, referencing the local beer.

I sat there, trying to listen to my own body, and shook my head. "I'm not really feeling it yet."

"Huh," he said, then looked at the vial. He started laughing. "Oh, just a kiddin', that was the saline." He pushed off the ground and rolled to the other side of the room, clearing out Ethiopian nurses in his wake, spun, then stopped as he had before, just before a medicine cabinet, from which he procured another bottle. He pushed off powerfully, rolled across the room, spun and parked it beside me once again.

"Here, we try dis on for size." He injected me again. "Now you feeling like you've had a nice big Tusker?" he said.

"Yes," I said. He pulled the needle out of my arm, stuck it back into the bottle, drew more fluid, and re-inserted the needle back into my arm.

"Alright, you shoulda be feelin' like you had a whole case of Tuskers," he said, smiling to me.

I waited, then shook my head. "I'm feeling it a little."

"Damn!" he exclaimed. "You are a big guy, how much you weigh?"

"Uhhh, 265 pounds," I said, a bit surprised that he didn't already know this. I thought anesthesia was a precise science, but I was also feeling super relaxed. He jammed the needle back into the vial—yes, the same one—sucked out a bunch of fluid, then pulled out the needle and began to push the plunger forward. He sprayed a bunch of the medication onto my gown, complementing the blood the nurse before had sprayed me with previously.

He then shot me up. "You should be falling asleep in ten... nine... eight..." I relaxed in my bed as he did the countdown, sending up silent prayers to God that he would guide the surgeon's hand. "Two... one... zero...." He continued to stare at me, then back at his watch. As I remained conscious, he drew out more anesthetic from the vial and shot me up again. This one did the trick. I was out.

(3 hours and two power outages later)

I woke up out in the hallway feeling a bit bleary. Standing next to the bed was Edgar the medic, looking tired and a bit fed up.

"How're you feeling?" he asked.

Sensations began to return to my body. I was on my side, and I felt a dull aching pain at the front of my face. I touched my nose and it came away with blood.

"Ahh, my nose!" I said. A deep, throbbing, shooting pain, began to build that felt like muscle being shorn from bone. "And my ass," I gritted.

"Bro, it's like nine p.m. so I'm probably gonna head back to the team house here," Edgar said.

"Nine p.m.... how long did the surgery go for?" I said.

"Pretty long, bro. The power went out like twice during your surgery," Edgar said. He went for something in his pocket. "Oh, looks like your boss is calling you," he said, and handed me the phone. I saw the caller ID: Craig, my NCOIC. How kind of him to check in on me. I answered the phone and watched the medic as the Ethiopians wheeled me back towards my room. I tried to focus my mind through the overwhelming pain.

"Hello," I said.

"How're ya feeling?" Craig asked.

"Craig, they broke my fucking nose, and they cut out way more than they said. I can fucking feel it, it feels like shit," I told him.

"Uh huh, well you still sound pretty out of it to me. I'll come by and check on you in the morning. Later..." Craig hung up on me.

I was a bit stunned that apparently that was all the concern I warranted. I cursed them all under my breath and began to piece together what had happened in my mind. I was still a bit groggy from the anesthesia, but the pain was focusing my mind. I remembered everything up until the final shot of anesthesia. I pieced together that the Ethiopian staff must've flipped me onto the table face down hard enough to have caused the bloody nose that I was experiencing. I was fairly certain that the procedure had not gone exactly as planned, though I wasn't sure and still needed to hear from the surgeon. The pain was ratcheting up and I was feeling totally neglected by my team. I was alone in an African hospital and being wheeled down a dingy, flickering hospital hallway without a clear idea of what had happened to me. Though soon, pain became my only concern.

I was rolled into my room, and the nurse positioned a rolling bedstand next to me.

"How did the procedure go?" I asked.

"The doctor will come by in the morning to discuss it with you. Do not get out of bed, and use this pitcher to pee if you need to," the nurse said. She handed me a plastic pitcher, then promptly left the room.

I peed into the pitcher and wound up with the shallow receptacle sloshing the fluid back onto myself. Eventually the Ethiopian nurse returned carrying a large needle. She walked around my bed to my backside where I could not see her. I felt the blankets being moved, she jabbed a needle into my ass and shot something into my cheek. Whatever it was, it knocked me out.

(The next morning)

I woke up a bit groggy and sore, lying on my side. My piss bucket was full to the brim. I hit the nurse button for the third time in fifteen minutes. No one came, and I suspected that the button was inoperable.

Dr. Kapoor entered the room. Thank God someone still works here.

"Hello, I think we had an excellent operation. I had to cut out far more than anticipated. Would you like to see the pictures?" he asked me.

I sure would, I thought. Maybe that will set my mind at ease one way or another. "Yes, that would be great," I said. He then whipped out his smart phone, and excitedly browsed through his files until he found them.

WARNING: The following image is graphic and not suitable for all audiences, but there it is.

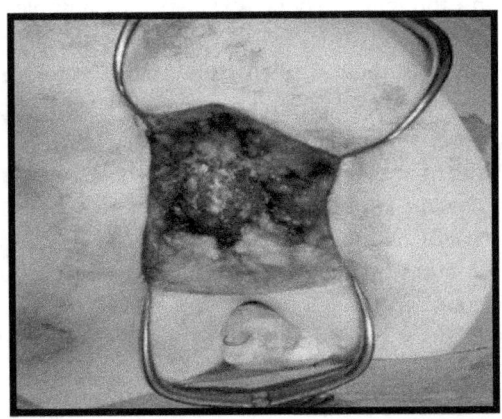

You see, I was still holding out hope that this had just been a small procedure, and that very little had actually been removed. I about barfed when I saw this picture, and the deep throbbing stabbing pain that permeated my ass and lower back suddenly became more sense. So did the realization that this guy paused midway through the surgery to whip out his cellphone (the same one he probably peruses the gram with when he takes a shit) and took a picture of it.

I was beginning to think this was his first time doing this and he was just super gung-ho about it all. He forwarded me the image through WhatsApp, and I promptly sent it on to my teammates (who still hadn't come by) on our group chat. I hoped that it would give them a better idea of the severity of my situation, but it didn't.

"You are going to be staying over here for a couple of nights and I will check in on you in the morning," Dr. Kapoor said quite pluckily. "Here is my contact information in case you need me." He handed me his business card and left the room.

His business card read: "Mr. Kapoor" not doctor—no M.D. or D.O. "Mr. Kapoor." My heart began beating in the back of my throat, and I thought surely he was just being humble or something on his business card. But it did raise some serious questions in my mind. I assured myself that I was simply overreacting. After all, a whole team of Tricare medical professionals had vouched for this guy, and hospital. My medic vetted him, and the embassy doctor approved of him. There was no way in hell this guy wasn't even a fucking doctor. Needless to say, the images of my surgery and the uncertainty of the status of whether or not Dr. Kapoor was Mr. Kapoor caused me to forget to ask him to empty my piss bucket.

I was left alone in the room with my very full bucket of piss, and my bladder was beginning to feel full again.

Eventually, a Ethiopian comes in and informs me that he needs to change the bedsheets and that I must get up. I explain to him that I can't get up, but he is adamant.

"That is nonsense," the nurse told me. "You need to get up. Here, let me help you." He grabbed my hand and tried to help me turn in my bed. Every movement was fucking agony. I gritted my teeth, though, and tried to turn on my side. Lying on my side without contacting my ass, I managed to get my feet down to the sticky linoleum floor. He began pulling me up. But I was a much larger man than Ethiopians were used to. His grip slipped and I slammed back into the bed, crumpling in agony. He relented.

"Perhaps I shall come by later then." He left me in the room without emptying my piss bucket. But frankly, I was in so much agony that I didn't really care.

(A short while later)

My teammates finally came by. Craig provided me with a Coke, then came around to the couch behind me. He discovered a dirty hypodermic needle lying on the couch, which he discarded. I told them about what was happening. They did me the courtesy of draining my piss bucket before taking off and telling me to text them if I needed anything. I needed a lot of things, which seemed patently obvious to me. And I'd made my concerns about the piss bucket, being dropped onto the bed, and being unsure if this guy was a doctor known to them. It all seemed to go in one ear and out the other. They spent most of their time with me complaining about the very little work they had to do.

And still, no one had addressed my post-op bloody nose. I'd still like to know what the hell happened there.

I was left alone in that African hospital for four nights and days, until eventually another teammate was sent to pick me up along with our chauffeur. I crawled into the back of the car, and we made our way back to the team house. I endured an extremely painful trip back upstairs and into my room, which was without A/C. Once there, I was essentially left, rarely checked on, and often without food. The whole time I didn't hear from anyone in the rear, higher echelons, my company commander, or first sergeant. This seemed a little odd to me, but I was assured that they were tracking the situation.

(Two weeks later)

I got my last layer of stitches removed, and I was told to be very careful with it. The stitch removal process was certainly less than fun. It involved me hobbling over to Jabali Hospital, into Mr. Kapoor's office, and lying down in his back office, which still smelled like curry, and having the old man cut and rip the stitches out of my ass wound.

By this point I'd determined that Mr. Kapoor was not a doctor in any sense of the word. My team was made aware, and most of them just found it comical. But they assured me that my wound looked good, and they expected me to be healthy soon.

Sure enough, though, I began bleeding out of my wound. Like, a lot of blood draining onto the bed. Naturally, I became alarmed by this and showed the medic, Edgar, the tons of blood that was leaking out. He studied it with his glazed eyes and assured me that was pretty normal.

Later, I developed a 103-degree fever and intense pain in my ass. I felt like I was going to die. I went to my officers' room and knocked on the door. He wasn't there—probably out with his dude friend. We all suspected that he was a closet homosexual, though none of us could figure out why he would be closeted still… we wouldn't care. Then I went to the NCOIC's room. I knocked on the door, and Craig slowly came out, wearing fresh cologne, obviously about to enjoy a night out with his Ethiopian girlfriend.

"Craig, I've got a fever of 103, and feel totally like shit."

He looked at me curiously. "You look like shit. When's your next doctor's appointment?"

"Tomorrow."

"Aight, go in tomorrow, and text me if you need anything." He walked past me to go violate a general order and bang some Ethiopian.

I went back to my room, a bit nervous about not waking up or having a major issue. I sent Craig a text telling him that my health was going south, and that I wanted him to make sure everyone in the rear knew what was going on. I wanted it logged as profile time, and to make sure that I was taken care of medically. He assured me that he would talk to our first sergeant about it. Reassured by these messages, I made it to the next morning and went to my appointment.

(Next day)

I arrived at Mr. Kapoor's office in a rather bedraggled state. I told him about the drainage, which he explained.

"This is a good thing. Nature is helping us!"

I got on the table, and he insisted on draining my wound. I looked over my shoulder and watched as he rummaged around his cabinet for supplies. He procured a bucket and a very large needle syringe. I lay on the table as he approached me, then proceeded to stab into what was now the healed-over scar tissue and into the wound. I writhed on the table as he moved it around and began sucking blood and pus out of the wound. By the time he was finished, he'd withdrawn 170 CC of pus out of my ass, which he proudly showed me in the bucket. He gave me a prescription for some antibiotics and told me to come back in two days.

My fever had died down and I returned to his office two days later, and continued leaking a significant amount of blood, and had to sleep on a towel. During this time, another special operations team arrived. Their captain and NCOIC saw me and became furious about the mistreatment, discovering that the rear command had never been informed about what had happened to me. A major shitstorm brewed, which led to a chain of events that would lead to me getting medevaced out of the country.

MY THIRD BUTT CHEEK: PART THREE

Things got heated and began moving pretty quickly after the rear found out that my NCOIC and OIC elected for me to have surgery in an Ethiopian hospital from a guy who wasn't a doctor, then proceeded to leave their soldier alone in a hospital in Al-Shabbab territory for four nights and days. Craig had tried deescalating the situation and told the 1SG that it'd been a real minor procedure and just a small cyst. That lie was discovered when the visiting team forwarded the 1SG pictures of my wound and grizzly surgery. He was a bit more than pissed at them.

I was quickly medevaced out of country. This didn't line up perfectly, though, and I found myself lying on a little stretcher in the back of a passenger plane going to Somalia. The visiting team said au revoir to me in Mogadishu, and from there I flew to Djibouti, where Navy medical guys greeted me. They waited for me on the tarmac, let me ride in the back of their truck, and took me to see a surgeon on post.

The surgeon looked at my wound and told me that it looked fine. She'd apparently spoken with Mr. Kapoor. She explained to me that she felt bad that the surgeon, Mr. Kapoor, thought us Americans didn't trust his work, and that she was worried that the whole thing was being blown out of proportion and was a result of some kind of implicit racism. At the time I didn't see through her woke bullshit and took her word for it.

I still had an open wound, mind you, and I'd been instructed to keep the thing as sterile as possible. The medical team there had assured me that I would be provided hygienic lodging with a personal shower. I would have to stay there a couple of days before I could catch a flight to Germany.

A Navy medic brought me to my lodging. He parked the UTV on the gravel in between rows of vertically stacked CONEX Boxes. On Camp Lemonier these had been outfitted with A/C and served as barracks for the soldiers, sailors, and airman stationed there. He gave me the keys and a trash bag full of sheets and wished me goodnight before speeding off.

I opened the CONEX box and discovered it to be epically ratfucked. There was food and discarded trash everywhere, as well as what I discovered to be mounds of pubic hair spread out across the floor beneath the bed to the sink and bathroom area. I'm not talking about a few stray hairs stuck here or there on the sticky floor; I'm talking about comically obscene clumps of it throughout. The next thing I did was try to put the sheets on the bottom bunk of the bed, and as I did so, wadded up and either sneezed or cummed in tissue paper fell from the top mattress and other odd places where the previous occupant had stuffed it between the frame and mattress of the top bunk. It rained down like some kind of unholy snow shower. I did my best to clean it up without any cleaning supplies at my disposal.

The bathroom was no better, as the previous occupant had obviously had explosive diarrhea, as evidenced by the violent splatter on the back of the toilet, as well a penchant for mycology based on the thick fungal bodies that resided in my "hygienic" shower area. I took a video of the whole place and sent it to my bosses, making them aware of the very real risk of my sustaining another infection. They told me to hold tight. I was stuck on this base without a ride, without assistance, without knowing where anything was, and without documentation that would allow me to dine in the chow hall. But at least the Army was "making sure" I was okay.

A day later, a fellow special operations guy came to my rescue. He helped me clean the place up, since I was unable to do much of it myself, being just about four weeks out from my surgery and still experiencing pain and discharge. He was disgusted and took pictures of it too. He formed a hypothesis about the identity of the enthusiastically masturbating, fungi growing, explosive shitting, pubic hair trimming, Pizza Hut-eating previous occupant. We suspected that this location had been previously occupied by one of the local terps. We hoped that perhaps it was beard hair, but more than likely, there was some sort of manscaping involved.

A day or two later, they put me on a flight to Germany. I was assured that it was going to be a comfortable medical flight out, with a place for me to stretch out, since I was still hobbled and absolutely could not put pressure on my still healing, open, and leaking wound. My 1SG and medics in the rear in particular were worried about having an attending medical professional on the flight, since they thought it was possible I might have some cavities or pustules under the surface that could potentially burst at higher altitudes.

It turned out that the medical team on Djbouti was full of shit. There were zero medical personnel. It was a cargo plane carrying a Humvee and pallets full of supplies. The best the aircrew could manage was to lower a bench and jam me between the piles of shit they had on board. It was a bumpy and rough flight. Every time the plane jolted, I feared the chained down Humvee would break loose and crush me to death. Furthermore, the only place to pee was at the backside of the plane, and to get there I had to shimmy my way past the Humvee, then literally climb over a pallet of metal, then jump down the other side. During the turbulent, long flight from east Africa to Italy, I had to make this trip several times, feeling my poor ass get brutalized by the proceedings, only to stand on a small platform to pee in front of the strange aircrew who laid in hammocks or sat Indian style on the pallet. They all looked in my direction as I did my business.

I arrived in Germany on a cold day early in the morning. Some guys from my unit picked me up and took me from Rammstein to the medical hospital. There was some wounded warrior housing that they stuck me in, for which I felt somewhat ashamed of using, but also grateful for.

Their Air NCOs managed me the next day and gave me a whole checklist of items that I had to accomplish before being allowed to board a flight back home for America. It involved being cleared and seen by a bunch of useless people who weren't the least bit helpful to me. It involved a surgeon giving me my prognosis without her ever even looking at it. There was also one incident where I was having CAC card issues and the air NCO said, "We've got an office that can fix that for you."

I responded, "Probably not," and the Master Sergeant got sassy with me.

"Of course we do, let's go right now."

So we get there and their CAC card machine is broken (as they always are) and I was proven right. At which point he just left me (my ride), without a car, phone or even knowing where I was on the unfamiliar German base. Not to mention there was a snowstorm, and I was fresh out of Africa, not exactly dressed for the occasion.

Regardless, I hobbled through the snowstorm, blinded, in the direction of what I believed were the wounded warrior barracks. Disturbingly, I was not the only person that I saw who had been abandoned. There are a couple of others who were in far worse shape, such as having stepped on an IED or something, and were left to fend for themselves traveling across the massive hospital, making bullshit appointments, and left to navigate a snowstorm too. Luckily though, I made it back to the barracks.

Eventually, I was able to get a flight back to the US aboard a C17.

I had three bags that I'd brought with me to Africa, one of which was laden with body armor and other Army equipment. I was told that on this C17 I could have no more than two thirty-five pound bags. This meant that I had to choose which bag to leave behind with my guys. It would be on them to figure out how to get it home for me. This, by the way, was a ridiculous proposition, as a C17 can carry ten Humvees, three Strikers, or one fifty-five ton Abrams tank across the Atlantic Ocean. But somehow a third bag would've caused a C17 only carrying a dozen patients and few medical staff to crash into the Atlantic. DoD logic at its finest. Again, I was told I would be given a stretcher because I couldn't sit on my ass, because I had ass surgery! And again, this was ignored, and I endured a very painful and uncomfortable ride on a rock-hard bench, alongside some kid who was being sent home early because he had "anxiety."

Finally, back in the good ol' US of A, on con leave, at home with my fiancé, I was admitted to the surgical clinic where I had regular appointments. They were tracking my injury and trying to determine if they could get it to heal, or if another surgery would be required. After a couple weeks of this, and me beginning to shit blood, the arrogant surgeon determined that I probably needed surgery. A date was set.

I was on a pre-op table. The surgeon came by and was going to mark up the wound for surgery. He looked at the wound.

"Hey, I think your wound site looks good, I don't want to perform a surgery. I'm going to cancel it." So the surgeon cancelled the surgery.

Then the next day, I violently shit blood again into a toilet. I returned to the surgeon a couple of days later, and he said, "Yes, you've got an infection and a cavity in there somewhere. We definitely need to do surgery."

"How soon can you get me in?"

"Probably late August."

"My wedding is at the end of August."

At this point I was pretty pissed, I'd been waiting months to get this surgery with this guy, with months of a documented lack of progress. He'd seen the records that I'd had massive infections and 170 CC of pus pulled out of my ass. I knew I had a cavity; why no else would believe me and none of these so-called experts could see it was beyond me. Some people kept suggesting to me that it was hemorrhoids, which I was tested for and found not to be the cause.

Anyways, I raised a ruckus, and tried to get a referral to a civilian hospital. Say, one of the world class ones like Duke, Wake, UNC, or many of the other topnotch hospitals that were within a two-hour drive from that location. But I got denied. I had to file a complaint against the doctor and articulate that'd I'd lost confidence in him.

I got denied. The general surgery team denied the request because they were staffed with sixteen "top notch" surgeons. Another surgeon called me. He seemed confident, humble, and had a good bedside manner. I asked if he wanted to get some imaging done to determine the size of the issue. He said that was unnecessary, as it would be a simple procedure. I decided to give him a chance, and he scheduled me in for a couple weeks later, which facilitated me attending my own wedding. The surgeon explained that he was going to perform a rhomboid flap procedure, that I would be left with just a little scar that kinda looked like a lightning bolt.

♦

The day had come. I awoke from the surgery with two vacuums running from my posterior. The surgeon came into my room and said, "There was a lot more infection on the inside than we were expecting."

"Like I've been telling you—and everyone else who's been involved in this—the entire time."

"Don't worry, we got all of it, and I think it'll heal well." I tried to get a picture of my ass with my phone but found that I was unable to get to it. It was covered in gauze and tubes. But thankfully this time I had received medication so I wasn't feeling too much pain. After a day, I was discharged.

♦

Eventually I went back to the hospital to have the bandages removed. They replaced the bandages with more temporary ones which they instructed me to change regularly.

I returned home, and it was time for me to change my own bandages for the first time. I stood up and went to a tall mirror so I could apply the bandages. That was the first time I saw my ass without the gauze on it and, oh boy, did I freak out. I now had three butt cheeks.

WARNING: The following image is graphic and not suitable for all audiences, but there it is.

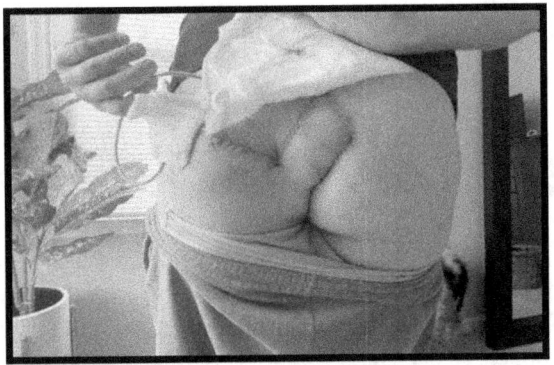

So much for just having a "little scar that will look like a lightning bolt." Thank God the Army had taken care of me. But alas, this story was not over. Subsequent MRI and ultrasound results revealed that there were still open pockets and probable infection beneath the grafted tissue. This time I filed several complaints through several people, and had a 1SG, CSM and a Lt Col all file complaints on my behalf too. Still, general surgery denied my request for a second opinion elsewhere. Finally, after further cajoling and leveraging of the chain-of-command, they relented.

This really goes to show that, no matter how much you bust your ass, work your tail off, get your rear in gear, or even kiss ass, the Green Weenie will fuck you. It fucked me so hard, it literally changed the geometry of my ass, and even years later it still hurts to sit! Being in the Army is a pain in the ass, literally. Perhaps you think that I'm just being cheeky. But the whole experience really chapped my keister. I'm glad that I left it behind. If you're in the Army, here's some advice: Cover your ass, no ifs, ands, or butts about it.

DEATH SHIT

It was four days since my second ass surgery, and five days since I'd pooped. I'd been taking a variety of laxatives every day to no avail. Finally, I felt something moving in my colon, and the poop that I'd been wanting as well as dreading seemed to manifest itself. With my fresh surgical scars and brand new third butt cheek, I wasn't sure how this was supposed to work. After all, I wasn't even supposed to sit down. But I knew that I would have to and that it would be extremely painful.

Finally on the Fourth of July, the urge to poop came. I slowly got up and out of bed, grabbed my blood satchel, and two blood vacuums that went into different parts of my ass and hobbled over to the bathroom. I inspected the lid, carefully lowered my shorts, and delicately (and painfully) lowered myself down to the toilet seat. All situated, cleared for lift-off.

Oh so gently did I begin to push. I could feel the poop coming into my lower rectum, and a pressure building within me, pressing against the wound from the inside out. Easy goes it, I thought. Just before it dislodged from my inner sphincter and broke through the point of no return, it ceased to move. I very cautiously gave an impish push, trying not to apply too much pressure to my damaged ass. But still, it didn't budge.

I thought that perhaps with time, it would move. I could feel it chambered, and about to go. It was just cresting the inner sphincter, and I could already tell it was a really hard poop, which surprised me because I had drunk liters of laxatives. For twenty minutes I toiled, but without success. I was beginning to sweat pretty hard and consider my options.

An hour passed, and I was in incredible amounts of pain. My asshole was bleeding. My wound felt like it was being ripped apart. I was drenched in sweat. Desperate, I called the Tricare Nurse Advice Line, which a polite older woman with a singsong voice answered.

"Hello, I can't poop and I've just had ass surgery. I have a third butt cheek. What should I do?" I said.

"Uhh, what did you say? Wait, hold on a second," the nurse said. "Let me get your name and date of birth."

"It's Joe..." I struggled to give her my name as I was experiencing what felt like contractions about to rip apart my asshole. "Lady, I'm in agony. What needs to happen here? Enema? Finger up the ass? What?" I said curtly.

"Well sir, just give me a minute to look some things up," the nurse said. Is she on WebMD? I thought.

"I swear to God, if you tell me pilonidal means nest of hair, lady..." I said.

"What?"

"Never mind. Lady, this poop is killing me, and the doctor told me not to strain too hard. Do I need to fuck myself with something to break this shit up? Tell me!" I said.

"Well..." she said, "you could try fingering it." I hung up on her, then felt myself slipping on the toilet lid, which was now slick with sweat. I decided to move to another bathroom. Perhaps another toilet will do the trick. I thought I could trick my mind into releasing this poop with a change of scenery.

"*Karen!*" I screamed, bellowing for my dutiful fiancée, who sat downstairs listening to her headphones, ignoring my plight.

"What?" she responded.

"I need a glass of water and more laxatives."

"More?"

"Yes! More!" I screamed. At least she would know what it was like to be on the receiving end when it came time for her to pass an unusually large and hard object.

My lovely fiancée came upstairs and into the bathroom in our bedroom. I must've been a sight, a sweat-soaked man, red-faced, sweating profusely, with veins protruding from my forehead, with two blood vacs sucking blood through tubes across the bathroom sink. I grabbed the water and Miralax and gulped it down like a man who's just found water in a desert. I put the glass down and strained some more.

Defeated by pain and dignity long since cast aside, I lathered my hand up with Vaseline and prepared myself to do the unthinkable. I reached up to find my virgin asshole, which proved more difficult than I would've thought, since the extra butt cheek was making it quite challenging to locate. Eventually I found purchase and thrust my finger into my ass hoping to find the blockage and break it up or remove it. It turns out fingering a hard piece of turd is quite unpleasant, and this caused even more pain.

I encountered something unusually hard and smooth. I inspected it as best as I could with my finger and, much to my dismay, it was hard as concrete.

"Karen!" I bellowed.

"What?"

"I think the surgeon left something inside my ass." In that moment of pain, I imagined the stellar Army surgeons had inserted a butt plug or something and had forgotten it. Of course, my fiancée challenged this.

"Why would they put a plug in your ass?"

"I don't know… maybe to keep me from shitting during surgery? I've got to get it out." I scratched at it with my finger and felt the thing budge inside of me. It was an extremely painful and laborious process, as I squatted and reached into my ass and desperately tried to extract the source of my profound misery. A few pieces came out but not the big score. But I succeeded in getting shit on my hand—I had flashbacks to RASP. My hand was too large, and I had a bad angle. I'm ashamed of what I did next.

"Karen! I need you to get a glove and help me!" I cried, nearly at the point of tears from this Luciferian turd.

"*What*?"

"Get a glove, lube up and pull this shit out!"

Sighing, she got up and started rummaging around for something. After what felt like an eternity, she emerged with some water-based lubricant and sandwich bags.

"Sandwich bags? What are we trying to do, save it for later?"

"We don't have gloves," she said.

I looked at the hard ridged Ziplock bags. "Alright, just don't lose a zipper in there," I said.

I bent over, providing Karen with an advantageous angle of infiltration. She reached in bravely, like a trooper, into her fiance's asshole like a fucking pro. I moaned as she moved around inside with the sandwich bag around her hand. She caused me to convulse with pain as she pinched at the impacted shit inside my ass. She managed to get just a few small pieces. She pulled out, threw the sandwich bag into the trashcan beside me. It smelled repugnant.

She did this again, but was unable to dislodge the poop. I sat back down, now more than two hours into the ordeal. "Karen, I need to get an enema. I need you to call 911."

"Okay," she said softly, and left with the unenviable task of calling 911 and explaining to them that her future husband couldn't poop. It would probably be the silliest call they received all day. But I didn't care. Dignity had long forsaken me. This poop had reduced me to a severely constipated man who'd just been fisted with a sandwich bag. I'd reached rock bottom. I considered suicide—not seriously. But I thought about it. Never had a turd so humbled me.

She made the call. From conversations after, I learned that this was the most awkward phone call that my fiancée had ever had to make. I really picked the worst day ever to have this kind of issue, since the Fourth of July is a holiday famous for its festivity-related injuries. I doubted I would even be able to get an ambulance out to our house. Moreover, how seriously would they take a call about a constipated guy?

"They're on their way," Karen said.

"No fucking way. I guess I'm not shit out of luck?" I said.

Karen just shook her head at me. With the ambulance on the way, I felt empowered to really get after this poop. After all, if I did tear my ass open, I likely wouldn't bleed out. So I pushed, toiled, and strained until my eyes bugged out of my head. I about passed out, but still, the fucker wouldn't budge. I would have to face the judgement of the paramedics.

Fifteen long minutes later, I heard the sirens outside. At least they were making sure that all my neighbors were aware that something was going down at our household.

"Joe, they're here," Karen yelled, like I didn't already know. I pulled up my pants and stood upstairs, collecting my blood bags, wallet, and other things that I knew I would need. The paramedics came into the room and saw me, covered in sweat, shaking, with two blood tubes coming out of my ass. I know I looked like an absolute train wreck.

"So we understand that you've been having some issues."

"Yeah, I can't poop, and had a surgery on my ass three days ago. I'm in a lot of pain, I need to get an enema or something. Also I think they might've left something in my ass."

"Oh, we understand. When you can't poop it's a big problem," one of them said to me, like they were some weird kid's educational show. I had never been more keenly aware of this scientific fact until that particular moment.

After very little cajoling, I hobbled down the stairs and to the front door of my home. They met me on the front porch where they insisted on putting me onto a stretcher. This was awkward for them since I couldn't lie flat on my back (due to my ass surgery) and had to hold my two blood vacuum devices. They carried me the rest of the way—dramatically—for all of my neighbors to see.

They must've been so concerned for me; already in my head I was thinking of stories to concoct for them. How could I face them again if they knew that I was being carried out on a stretcher because I couldn't poop? I would become the laughingstock of the neighborhood.

It was a long and bumpy ride to the hospital. The ambulance seemed to hit every curb, sending nasty, painful ripples through my body with each jolt. It felt like someone had shoved a glass chandelier up my ass and then smashed it repeatedly with a hammer. By the time we arrived, I was in utter agony. I needed this poop out STAT. But of course, the administration section at the hospital had other intentions.

"Alrighty sir, what's a good home telephone number?"

"How about a cell phone?"

"Next of kin?"

"Address of next of kin?"

"Alternative address?"

"What's your favorite color?" I'm making this one up of course. I was losing my patience but unfortunately not losing my shit.

"Lady, I need this dealt with now! Can we do this later?" The answer to this question was a resounding no, and I had to answer her stupid questions. I wondered if the gunshot victims tonight would have to jump through the same hoops. "Sorry, sir, can you repeat that first part?"

"*gurgle* *gurgle*"

I was brought back to my room. Once the nurse got me settled, she brought back a doctor, a short, pallid fellow with a droopy, cranky expression. He asked me about my surgery and what I'd been feeling and I told him. I had a fecal impaction... that I'd felt it. He concurred but decided that we should do x-rays before proceeding.

"But I don't know why you came here; you got really lucky we could bring you back here. You should've gone to the hospital on base for this."

"I came here because I knew I wouldn't have to wait long. It was closer, and Army hospitals suck."

"Like I said, you got lucky."

"I got lucky last time too."

"You should've gone somewhere else."

"Well, I guess I'm going to keep coming here as long as I'm lucky," I said as this doctor with an agenda tried to lecture me in between bouts of fruitless but imminently painful contractions. He left after a bit, and I lay in the room waiting for the X-rays for what felt like forever. I just wanted relief.

A nurse came in to check on me. "Excuse me, can we just do the enema and get this poop out?" I asked.

"Not before we do the X-ray."

Eventually, the X-ray lady came in and discovered that she couldn't get a good X-ray of me, because I couldn't get into the "correct position" due to my ass surgery.

"I guess we'll just have to forgo the X-ray then," she said. Apparently, I'd waited for nothing. A kinder nurse came in and set up a flimsy-looking and quite shallow bedside commode. She left before returning with a container full of warm soapy water, the enema.

"Sir, would you like your fiancée in here for this?"

"To watch me shit? I think I'll pass." She shrugged her shoulders, filled up the bag, and had me turn over. She shoved the lubed tube into my ass and had to ram it back and forth to get through the fecal impaction. It hurt like hell, but at least I knew relief was coming.

I felt the warm fluid fill up my lower intestines, and the urge to go came.

"Alright, clench your sphincter and try to hold in the fluid," she said, as she withdrew the enema tube from my ass. Immediately I knew I had to go. I lurched out of the bed, shambled across the small room with my blood vacs in hand, and lowered myself onto the commode.

Then I pushed.

Warm liquid came streaming out, and I pushed harder, fearing that this measure was failing. But then it moved. Oh, I felt glorious movement. It slipped out of position and began to breach my asshole and kiss the hospital air. I felt my asshole widen, horribly widen. It ripped my ass as it shot out into the tiny commode vigorously. Then it kept coming. I kept violently shitting. A foul stink filled the air. I worried that my third butt cheek would tear from the strain.

The kind nurse left out of sheer panic.

The shit kept coming, hard knotted shits, and I could tell my asshole was bleeding. It reminded me of the South Park episode where Randy Marsh takes the biggest shit in the world, beating Bono's record.

But regardless, sweet relief was mine.

I felt an odd calm, like the calm after the storm, or the calm one feels after surviving a pitched and protracted battle, with the overwhelming feeling of joy at finding oneself intact and alive. I stood up from my commode—my throne of victory—to inspect the aftermath.

It was truly impressive; what I pooped looked unnatural, alien, and unlike any other poop that I'd known before.

It was hard and deep dark black. It had retained its shape despite being bashed against the hard-plastic walls of the pan. It was an impressive poop, to say the least, topping even my NC state dorm room poop. I swore to myself that from that day forward I would eat a lot of fiber. Perhaps I would become a brand ambassador for Raisin Bran Crunch.

The door slid open behind me and roused me from the afterglow of victory. I turned and saw the nurse standing there. With one hand she sprayed a can of Febreze, with the other she pinched her nose. I laughed, triumphant as I might be—exposed in my breezy hospital gown, glowing over a much too full commode. I felt slightly embarrassed, but mostly relieved.

"Can I go now?" I asked.

I hobbled out, toting my blood vacuums and looking like a bag-of-ass. My concerned fiancée waited for me in the waiting room. She pulled the car around to the front and opened up the back hatch so I could crawl into the back. Dusk was setting, and we drove home as the Fourth of July fireworks began volleying and alighting the night with the majestic colors of freedom.

PART 5
WEIRD-ASS ROOMMATES

MY WEIRD ROOMMATE #1: SPIDERMAN

It was late on a Friday night, and I'd just arrived to my unit. My new NCO had told to me find someone on CQ and have them take me to my new room. I stood out front of my new barracks. I grabbed a single bag from the back of the Honda, inside of which was stuffed all of my worldly possessions. I decided that I would get the rest tomorrow. Right now, I just wanted to sleep.

Before me stood my new barracks, a stark, concrete structure, at the front of which was a tin metal portico, lit by flickering lights. Apart from the large cockroaches outside, there were no signs of life. Cautiously I walked inside and saw a counter behind a window. I recognized this as the CQ desk, a position that was supposed to be attended 24/7 by an NCO and a junior enlisted. Their job was both to protect and assist the barracks residents.

The post was unattended. Behind the messy desk was a common room, illuminated by TV static. I set my bag down and waited a few minutes.

Growing impatient, I went behind the CQ desk and looked for the barracks management book. I'd worked CQ for another unit and knew that they usually kept a folder with lists of barracks rooms and assigned personnel. I found a white folder and searched for my name amongst the first-floor rooms. Surprisingly, the record book had been updated, and I found my name (albeit misspelled). I went out, grabbed my two overly stuffed green duffle bags, and headed to my room.

As unwelcoming as the vacant entrance had seemed, things got worse as I went down the corridor. I passed by a dark and moldy-smelling laundry room and saw someone inside of it; by the glint of their glasses, it appeared the dark silhouette was staring at me. Just wanting to get to my room without incident, I avoided eye contact.

I pushed through a pair of double doors that led into a long hallway. The hallway had a lurid ambience imparted by the decaying mold that clung to the light fixtures. In the dark recesses, more roaches scuttled about. I passed an older man, early forties, presumably a divorcee, who sat comatose, with his back to a barracks door. When I eventually located my room, I was unhappy to see that it was adjacent to a locked door with an unidentified machine groaning behind it. I jangled the key quickly from my pocket and eased the door open.

The door opened up to a small barracks common area with a fridge, stovetop, sink, and a small high-top table with two tall stools. Behind the common area were two doors that led to two private bedrooms. The place wasn't dirty per se, but rather had so long ago absorbed the filth that the filth became endemic to its structure, perhaps vital to its integrity. The linoleum floors seemed to have absorbed the clay, the ventilation had mildew, half of the griddles didn't work, and the temperature was stuck at 62 degrees. Not bad by army barracks standards. I'd certainly stayed in far worse conditions.

The door to the occupied room opened, and a short, ginger guy wearing a tie dye shirt emerged. He stood at his door and looked at me blankly.

"Hey, my name is Joe. Just arrived to the unit. I was told this is my room," I said.

"Maybe… no-one lives in that room," he said, pointing to the other room.

"Well, that works for me. I didn't catch your name?" I said.

"I didn't say it."

"Oh, well... what's your name?"

"Chase," he said.

I put my bag down, crossed the room and shook his hand. He looked at my hand, as if this was some exotic and bewildering custom.

"Nice to meet ya, man," I said.

"Yeah." In addition to his curt replies, I noticed that he hadn't blinked. "So where ya from?" I asked.

He answered.

"Oh, that's cool, I hear that's a pretty fun place to live," I said.

"It isn't," he said.

"Haha... yeah... so you like it here?"

"No," he said.

It was obvious that he wasn't the greatest conversationalist, so I tried to excuse myself. "Hey man, it's getting late, and I need to put my shit up. Great meeting you," I said, then turned to move my bag.

"I'm pretty autistic." He threw it out there like he'd been waiting to tell someone for a long time. I paused. I wasn't sure how to respond to this, but that would certainly explain the short conversation. I decided to be as diplomatic as I could about it.

"I could see that." I said, "But lots of people are autistic, it's okay to be socially awkward, bud." He looked wide-eyed for a minute. I began to wonder if he was going to lick his eyeball like a lizard.

"No, I said I'm *artistic*. Want to see my art?" he said. Now I felt like a jackass and obligated to say, "Absolutely." He invited me into his room for a tour.

It was a very colorful room. Around the perimeter against the upper trim, he'd strung programmable LED lights that faintly strobed. Beneath these, he had various pieces of trippy, psyche-delic art. Among the spiraling neon universes, there were a monkey wearing sunglasses seeing God for the first time, vortexes, repeating geometric drawings (of his own design), nude women, some action figures and video game art, a giant flatscreen television, futon, and a huge gaming computer with a water pump that pushed fluid through it like it was some kind of cyborg. More interestingly than his decorum, he also had a terrarium sitting on his windowsill with turtles, frogs, and other random creatures he'd caught outside, which was visible from the outside at ground level and very against regulation. Additionally, there were some potted plants, especially cacti, one of which he informed me was in fact a peyote plant that he'd acquired online.

"Oh yeah, by the way, I like drugs," he said nonchalantly.

"Nice," I said, still feeling like an ass about before.

"Yeah, wanna see the shrooms I'm growing?" he asked, like a kindergartener asking his dad to look at the pictures he's drawn.

"Ummm... sure?" I said.

He took me to his closet, inside which there were more terrariums and little greenhouses with mushrooms, in fact, growing inside of them. "Yeah, these bad boys should be done here in the next couple of days. Then I'm gonna have to dry them out. I'm thinking about doing that in the oven, then maybe giving them some sunlight, which I could put on the window sill—" He kept talking, and my mind was blown. We were subject to very frequent and random room inspections, since we fell under UCMJ. Any of the things he had just shown me would be career enders. You could get an Article Fifteen for just keeping pets in the barracks, never mind growing your own psychedelic shrooms and cacti. When I thought it couldn't get any worse, he revealed his venomous spider collection.

"This one is a brown recluse. I actually found it on a wall in the hallway. The black widow" —he said, holding up another small terrarium—"I found out in the motor pool beneath a pallet of wood."

I wondered if I could get in trouble for just being associated with this guy. I was also gravely concerned that my druggy roommate would get bitten playing with one of his pets while high.

"Oh yeah, you'll like this. You seem like a gun guy, right?" he said.

"Sure am," I said.

From behind one of his terrariums, he procured a fully loaded, and I must say, very nice, AR-15. Real primo shit. This is also not something one is allowed to have in their barracks room. He handed it to me, and I momentarily forgot about the poisonous spider and drugs admiring the sleek lines and lightness of his gat.

"Bro... how do you have all of this shit in here?"

"What d'ya mean?" he said, looking at me with wide, confused eyes.

"We're subject to random room inspections... right?"

"Yeah, but I've never had it happen, plus I'd just hide it," he said.

"Where would you hide your terrariums, peyote, shrooms, greenhouse, and this?" I pointed to the AR-15 in my hand.

"I'd just go stick it in my car," he said. I nearly laughed at the image of him, sneakily running out to his car with an AR-15 and several large terrariums, plus whatever other ungodly shit he had in that room.

"Well, I'm glad you're confident about it," I said.

"Yeah, there's nothing to sweat about," he said. "In fact... wanna get high tonight?"

"Not really, thank you though."

"Well... I've been reading that if you take enough Robitussin you can in fact get high."

"Robitussin?"

"No, it's true, it's called robo-tripping. If you do about four bottles worth, it'll send you to the fucking moon," he said.

I could definitely tell that drugs had melted this dude's brain. "Won't that kill you? Four whole bottles?"

"No." He shook his head. "It takes a lot to OD."

"I feel like four bottles is a lot."

"I'll be fine. So are you in or not?"

"I'm good, dude, but I appreciate it."

I went back into my room, and began unpacking my shit, processing my interaction with my new roommate. He was breaking an ungodly number of rules, laws, and regulations, and I wondered if I could somehow be found culpable. I decided that I was probably fine. I didn't know for sure what that shit was. Maybe this was a crazy prank for newcomers, like a shit test to see if you'll rat on your battle buddy. Besides, if it was real, I didn't want to piss him off.

A short while later, there was a knock at my door. I opened it, and Chase and his unblinking eyes looked up at me. He held a shopping bag full of bottles up next to his head proudly.

"Hey man, I'm about to get lit. You sure you don't wanna join?"

"I'm positive."

"Well... alright... you at least wanna see me down 'em?" he asked.

I contemplated this for a few seconds. "Sure, why not." We moved into the common room, and he laid out four bottles of liquid Robitussin.

"Bro, I should be robo-tripping hard," he said excitedly. He began cracking the bottles open, one by one, and poured himself a tall glass of orange juice. "Well, without further ado," Chase said, and began chugging his first bottle. I was expecting him to spew, as I knew that shit didn't taste good, but Chase didn't seem to be affected. He went through three more bottles like a fucking animal. He burped and washed it down with orange juice.

"Ahhh, that wasn't so bad," he said.

I was expecting magic, or for him to drop dead, but nothing of the sort happened.

"Anyways..." Chase glanced down at his watch. "I'm probably gonna go to my room and start playing video games. Gonna be a minute before it kicks in. Enjoy the rest of your night!" Chase walked into his room and closed and locked his bedroom door behind him.

I was stunned by what I'd just witnessed. A short while later, I heard laughter and the sounds of explosions coming from his room. An hour after that, silence ensued other than the theme music playing from the loading screen of a video game. I knocked on his door and got a groan in response. At least I knew he was alive, though I was unsure of what kind of state he was in. This guy was putting me into a hell of a situation, particularly during my first night at my new unit. After all, it wouldn't be a good look if my roommate died our first night together. The barracks conspiracy culture would go into hyperdrive. I would be put under investigation, and even after I'd been absolved, I would forever be known as the "roommate killer." Concerned, I turned to Google to determine what kind of predicament I was actually in.

After some research, I determined that the chance of Chase dying was low. I took a breath, relaxed, and unpacked my shit. I tried to forget that my new roommate was a complete psycho. And made the most out of my first night of privacy in years.

Of all the things I'd been presented with by this weird roommate, it was the spiders I felt most threatened by. WTF?

MY WEIRD ROOMMATE #2: CHOIRBOY

During PSYOP 'tryouts', I'd taken it upon myself to assign everyone on my team a nickname. Booger Sugar was a strait-laced and deeply religious black guy. Monkey Butt was an Asian guy with a rashy ass. Whore was a white guy who spent more time with other teams than with us. Hawk-Eye was some guy with absolute shit vision. Pizza was a guy who'd fucked a fat chick in exchange for pizza. Mom was an epically jacked lesbian. Sleep-douche was a dude who cursed out people in his sleep. During bag dumps the cadre had found a box of condoms in Magnum's bag. Dr. Strange was some dude who looked just like Benedict Cumberbatch. Last but not least, Choirboy was an uptight, prudish, Goody Two-shoes. My nicknames stuck, so much so that we didn't even know each other's real names. Even the cadre referred to us by the nicknames I'd assigned everyone.

I was convinced I would get DQ'd for the slightly racist nicknames. But I didn't—in fact, I peered extremely well, and the board selected me.

I returned to the 82nd, back to my NCOIC and 1SG (who'd deliberately tried to sabotage me with CQ-duty the night before selection). I happily informed them that I would be moving onto to greener pastures, and that I'd been one of the top performers at selection. They were not pleased. I believe the 1SG referred to me as a "pussy."

Given the toxic climate of the 82nd, I was all too happy to move on with my life.

First, the ARSOF recruiter rescued me and got me paperwork so that I could do on the job training, which consisted of me not going to morning PT with my unit and instead fucking off with the recruiter. It was outstanding.

Shortly thereafter, my orders came down, and I packed up my 82nd barracks room. I said sayonara to my piece of shit roommate and moved down the street to even shittier barracks.

During the qualification course, aspiring PSYOP soldiers were quartered at a barracks room in a corner of Fort Bragg known as "Smokebomb Hill." Years ago, before the Army got soft, Smokebomb Hill became so named because cadre used to bust down the doors of would-be special operations soldiers by throwing smoke bombs and tear gas into the barracks rooms for impromptu PT sessions. Though SOF's budget is large, none of it has been used to upgrade the student barracks. They are black-mold ridden, insulated with asbestos, rusty plumbing pipes in carcinogenic water—and they have biblical infestations. Let's talk about the infestation issues.

You see, there is a delicate ecosystem that exists on Smoke Bomb Hill. It would seem that the lowest layer of the food chain is the SOF student. Their trash and filthy habits form the base substantive layer, equivalent to the scum at the bottom of a typical food chain. From there we have the pigeons, who feed on the trash and filth of the privates. These pigeons alternate between consuming the alley food and defecating into the alley from their roosts. At the top of the food chain are the cockroaches. The cockroaches feast on the bird shit and sick pigeons, dragging what little remains there were of the garbage into the crevices.

I remember discovering this my first night at the barracks. The guys and I were outside and had just had a competition to determine who could pee the highest—I got my ass kicked by Smith, who sprang like a gymnast then whipped his dick back, sending sparkling droplets at least twenty feet into the air. After this defeat I went into a nearby alley to piss some more. We'd been chugging Busch.

In the dark, I heard scuttling. I pulled out my phone and turned on the flashlight. The light revealed a rolling sea of black carapace. Roaches clamored over one another, devouring shit, trash, and each other.

From private, to pigeon, to cockroach, the circle of Smoke Bomb life went on.

As unpleasant as the situation was for me, it was absolutely maddening to my new roommate, who was none other than my teammate from selection, Choirboy. Choirboy was as strait-laced as they came.

Choirboy's religion was order. Everything on his desk was in neat little rows. He made his bed every morning. He woke up at 4:30 a.m. seven days a week, so that he could read the news, hand grind his own coffee, then go through his yoga routine, while listening to some motivational bullshit. He epitomized discipline and generally had his shit pretty together. He was always the most well rested, limber, and hydrated motherfucker in the battalion. His side of the room reflected these tendencies: clean, bright, white, and organized.

My religion was chaos. My side was dark, filthy, and strewn with dirty clothes and unspeakable things. I would roll out of bed thirty minutes before formation, pick clothes out of a wrinkled pile, rip a cigarette, then go to morning PT still hungover.

The aesthetics of my side of the room weighed heavily on him, as did other features of our living space.

Every couple of days, the back of the toilet would be covered in dark, suspicious looking spots and splats. Choirboy assumed it was my fault.

"Dude, do you keep shitting in the toilet?" Choirboy asked.

"Yes, I poop in the toilet. If you want, I can use the sink instead," I said.

"No, gross. What I meant was that there's always shit stains on the back of the toilet," Choirboy said.

"I assumed that was your 'clean diet,'" I said.

"No, bro, I don't have health problems."

"I don't have health problems... yet," I said.

"Well, it's okay if you don't want to fess up to it, but I know it's you, bro," he said.

"Do you really believe that I just constantly have diarrhea and blow out the toilet every single day?" I said.

"Gluten gives a lot of people irritable bowel syndrome. I think you should get that checked out."

"I take healthy solid shits, thank you very much," I said.

Choirboy just shook his head. "Anyways, I'm done cleaning it up. If you make a mess in there, I'd appreciate it if you cleaned up after yourself."

"Sure," I said, entirely convinced that Choirboy was the one painting the porcelain black.

The next morning, the questionable material had returned. It spread outside of the toilet like an ectomorph. Finally, we concluded that it wasn't diarrhea, but rather some hitherto undiscovered bleach-resistant strain of black mold. I found it fascinating and thought that we should write a paper to unveil our discovery to the world. I imagined that scientists could harness the regenerative powers of the fungi.

Choirboy was less enthralled. He declared war on the thing. Many a night I would awaken to him gloved and going at it with the toilet, battling back both the fungus and gurgling backwash of shit water, only for the black mold to respawn overnight across the bathroom, from toilet to floor, to shower. He would wake up and begin an intensive chemical warfare campaign of Lysol and bleach. Many Geneva conventions were broken, and many fungi souls were lost. But it was a pyrrhic victory. Choirboy was spending a lot of money trying to clean the place, and the fungi kept spawning, and the toilet kept clogging. No matter how many times he bleached or cleaned it, no matter how regular his applications—it would not die. It was driving him to madness.

I laughed and provided absolutely no assistance, because he needed this. This was his burden to bear, his Sisyphean struggle to endure, and I refused to deny him it. But this mold was not to be the only issue with our room.

One day during a lunch break, I decided to go back to our barracks room. I made my way up the pigeon shit-covered stairs, stomped a few roaches on the balcony, then entered our room. Evidently, sometime between 0900 and 1130 the toilet had backed up and overfilled with shit water. I glanced in and saw some foul water bellowing out of the toilet and sloshing onto the linoleum floor. It was pooling inside the bathroom and beginning to seep out and move toward our beds.

I grabbed all the nearby towels and threw them into the rushing water that was coming out of the bathroom and into the common space. I shut off the water and tried to sop it up. But I was pressed for time and had to return to formation quickly. I hadn't even enough time to eat. I decided that I would clean up the rest after class.

The day wrapped up a bit later than usual. I trudged across the base, back to the barracks room, mentally preparing myself to clean up more sewer water. To my surprise, it had already been cleaned, and the room smelled like ferns in the spring. I turned to thank Choirboy for his service, but as I saw him, I immediately detected "angry spouse vibes." Choirboy sat in the dark, on a chair facing me from his half of the room. He didn't greet me or even ask the customary, "how was your day?"

"Thanks for grabbing that, man. It started leaking while I was leaving, and I started to mop it up but had no time to finish…"

"So you were just going to use my towel like that, were you?" His voice cut through like a hiss.

"I just grabbed what was nearby, man. I had to stop it from running to our bedroom area and equipment."

"Oh, it was just right there, was it? The towel that I clean my face and body with, just there, perfect for throwing into barracks *shitwater!*" he shouted. I tried to keep from laughing.

"It was an emergency, man. It was coming towards all of our gear. The towel did not die in vain," I said.

"It was a cashmere towel."

"Well shit, I'll get ya a new one," I said. Choirboy did not respond.

"I'll make this right man," I said. Zack… uh, that is, Choirboy, still didn't say a word. I was getting the silent treatment. Choirboy didn't even acknowledge me for the rest of the night, which was extremely awkward because our beds were about ten feet away from one another, without walls separating us. He was evidently very distraught about the fate of his cashmere towel. The next morning he didn't even get up and go through his daily yoga routine. Clearly the loss of the towel had broken his heart.

A couple of days later, I got him a new towel, but it didn't meet his exhaustive list of criteria; evidently, I'd sacrificed a very bougie towel. My efforts to reconcile were unsuccessful.

The way I looked at it, I'd acted on a critical situation with speed and aplomb and done everything I could to appease the victim (not sure if that was Choirboy or the towel). It didn't take long before I was getting fed up with Choirboy's shit. He would just sulk and bitch and moan every time I came home, about the roaches, the pigeons, the toilet, the black mold, the asbestos flakes that fell onto his face as he slept, the barracks bunny's loud fucking next door, guys peeing in the common area, the broken laundry machine that made clothes gritty, the carcinogenic barracks water… blah blah blah.

I loved this place and was frankly annoyed that he didn't appreciate the fine home the Army provided us. I had to remind him about all the soldiers in Africa who didn't even get barracks rooms and told him he should be more grateful. It wasn't just his constant complaining that irked me; it was also the fact that his lifestyle was being imposed upon me.

Overnight he would insist that the lights were off, and that he was tucked in by nine p.m., like we were living in a nursing home. Then, like clockwork, this well-rested cocksucker would wake up every morning at 4:30 a.m. to watch the news, hand grind his own coffee beans with some antique hand grinder that squeaked like a pornstar's mattress, and then boil water in a whistling kettle, before proceeding into a very sexually suggestive morning yoga routine.

Shirtless and in nothing but ranger panties, Choirboy would roll out his yoga mat, and 'limber up.' His stretches looked like they came from the Kama Sutra. He seemed to favor the downward dog and supine humping in particular, as he claimed to have very tight hip flexors.

Naturally, this irked me. I'd made some comments to him, but I think that this only encouraged him and he was passive-aggressively avenging his cashmere towel. Being an aspiring PSYOPer myself, I decided that I too would be passive-aggressive. Choirboy's most obvious weakness was his OCD. I started my psychological war campaign by randomly moving his shit around and disrupting his organized and delicate little OCD world. This upped his stress levels substantially.

"Where the heck is my coffee grinder?" he asked frantically one morning.

"I dunno, bro," I smirked.

This didn't deter him though, as he then decided to modernize and bought a very loud electric grinder. He'd won this round.

I knew that I had to up the ante. He finally had the mold under control. Luckily our mutual friend downstairs still did not. I paid our friend a visit and casually decided to use his bathroom. I unfolded a piece of wax paper that I had in my pocket and pressed it against the mold in order to get a spore print. I then returned to our room and seeded the spores along the inside of our toilet. Sure enough, it returned with a vengeance.

Choirboy bought more cleaning supplies and commenced the 2nd Mold War. I was incurring cost upon my enemy, but this still was not enough. He still persisted with his morning routine.

One day while he was stretching, I decided that I would broadcast to the world the abuse I had to endure. I filmed his routine, provided colorful commentary, and sent the videos out to all the other PSYOP students. This became known as "Choirboy Snaps."

Choirboy Snaps was a snapchat group that included all our friends and even Choirboy's little brother. Choirboy Snaps became pretty popular. Word got around and everyone wanted in on the group. The eccentric life of Choirboy fascinated people.

"Here we have Choirboy in the wild, stretching his hip flexors, in order to offset the stiffness that he incurs from being so uptight; he must stretch out every morning in order to relax his anus so that he can shit diamonds and ready himself for another full Choirboy day."

"Hey!" Choir said, looking at me from between his legs.

"Oh, crikey! Here we've got Choirboy hand grinding his pretentious coffee quite loudly at 0430! Like a rooster trying to beat the other roosters to the punch, hours before the crack of dawn!" I filmed from my bed across the room. "And now he's pissing like a racehorse with the door wide open for everyone to see!"

"What the fuck, man!" he said, as he clearly became self-conscious of his loud peeing.

"Here we have Choirboy, mouth wide the fuck open, trying to lure the flies in like a Venus flytrap!" I snapchatted him while he took his midday catnap.

Choirboy Snaps got to be pretty big. At formation people would ask me for an invitation to the group. Most of the battalion was part of the Snapchat group. In class and all throughout the day, they would poke fun at him. Choirboy became quite defensive of his lifestyle.

"It's called self-care. In thirty years, I'll still be limber as fuck, while all of you are hobbled!" he burst out once. This caused a lot of laughter, though in hindsight it was spot on.

My plan was working. Now, would Choirboy Snaps make Choirboy snap? I decided to apply more pressure in an effort to break him. Something very funny happened though.

"So how many people are watching your stupid snaps about me?" he asked, while in a Low Bow Pose.

"Thirty... give or take," I said.

"Whoa, just thirty, huh? You know, I think it has some potential."

"Are you saying we should get you an OnlyFans?"

"Well, you're along the right track. I was thinking more an Instagram page... you know, start making some money on this and showing my disciplined lifestyle," he said.

I contemplated it. "You know, that would probably work..." I said, somewhat surprised by his reaction.

"I think I could inspire a lot of people."

"You are so inspiring," I said, silently mocking him.

"Yeah, so I think I could make it a thing, you know, like Jocko Willink, get up extra early, show a picture of my watch, that kind of thing."

"That sounds fucking awful," I said.

"Well, you're already going to be up anyway, so we'll make it a thing," he said.

I decided right then and there to terminate Choirboy Snaps. He sucked all the joy out of it for me by embracing it. This guy was either totally naïve or he had outsmarted me.

In hindsight, he definitely used reverse psychology on me, and I'd fallen for it hook, line, and sinker. Touché, Choirboy.

PART 6
RANDOM ACTS OF DEGENERACY

BURNING MAN

While in AIT down in Fort Gordon.
    There we were, a regular bunch of 18X rejects. The guys who didn't make it. Everyone had their reasons, most of them bullshit. What we all shared was regret and pent-up frustration. Our morale took a hard nose dive when the Army—instead of honoring our original contracts and training—decided to reclassify all of us in accordance with "the needs of the Army." As it turned out, the Army badly needed signal support specialists, so me and about fifteen other guys got cut orders and got sent down to Fort Gordon to go through another AIT.

At least this time around, they gave us the prior service treatment, so we got our own barracks, were free to go where we wanted on the weekends, and weren't fucked with too bad. However, the barracks situation wasn't ideal. In fact, these barracks make my top five list of worst places the Army has ever stuck me.

These barracks were asbestos ridden. The building had been condemned and had cautionary signs posted all around. Because of the health hazards, they advised us to avoid nailing anything into the walls or messing with the drop ceiling, to filter our water, to avoid breathing inside the building too much... Avoid breathing inside the building? Like when we're sleeping? It was the usual Army bull. Rooms were two people to a room, with the beds oddly close together. As a part of a running gag, at the top of my desk and on full display, I kept an urn full of my dog's ashes, a book titled *Adolf Hitler,* portraits of some random old rednecks, a sword, and a squirrel figurine. I wasn't sure what I was trying to communicate to any would-be 1SGs doing an impromptu barracks inspection, but I hoped to make them as uncomfortable as they had made me (surprisingly my 1SG thought it was hilarious and sent pics of it to the command team, but that's a story for another time).

Anyway, there we were, a bunch of disgruntled reclassified soldiers undergoing a more technical portion of our signal training. Luckily, we had a long lunch break, and most of us elected not to go to the DFAC. Instead, we spent our time in the woods across the street from the classrooms.

The guys had started bringing hammocks, then because we were digging the campy feel, we dug out a fire pit and begun several major construction projects.

First, we built a treehouse; we sawed down trees, split wood, and fashioned rough 2x8s. We positioned them in the trees on sturdy branches about ten feet in the air and lashed them down with 550 chords. Next, we constructed a tomahawk throwing range with multiple tree stumps and made a very challenging course of it. While at it, we made some benches, which we placed around our fire pit. Within a few weeks, we had a full-fledged gypsy camp, which we ceremoniously christened "The Shire," and fashioned a sign marking the spot as ours.

One lunch period we'd all gone out and grilled brats and hung out, then returned to class, as usual.

Everything was perfectly ordinary and droll until sirens began blaring. We could tell that there were multiple vehicles parked just outside.

"I wonder if someone went down," a classmate said. Then there was knocking at our door, and an MP motioned for the instructors to step outside.

One of our classmates looked out the window. "Shit! There's a fire truck!"

"We put the fire out, right?" I muttered.

"Yeah, man, that thing was buried under sand," a classmate responded.

Things got even tenser after we spotted our first sergeant outside. "Oh, shit, we're fucked," someone said. Others muttered in agreement. Soon the door swung open.

"All you 18Xray motherfuckers better get the fuck outside and lineup!" the cadre said.

We got out of our seats and filed outside as quickly as we could, steeling ourselves for a good chewing and smoke session. Across the street we could see smoke billowing out of the woods. Two fire trucks were pulled up, and a very angry fire chief—and an even more pissed off first sergeant—leered at us.

"We're fucked," a classmate muttered.

We made a formation and hit the parade rest position. The first sergeant glared at us, his pupils dialed in like a fucking shark's. He was practically foaming at the mouth.

"I gave you stupid fucks too much rope… and God fucking damn it, you mother fuckers hung yourselves with it," he growled, pacing before us menacingly. "The base commander is going to be here any minute. He will decide your fate…" He stared each of us down and returned to a tense conversation with the fire chief.

The guy to my left gave me a nudge. I dared to look into the woods. I could see smoldering embers through the tree line. Fire fighters were going around with fire extinguishers. Right then, I knew that we weren't just fucked—we might even do some jail time, and the fact that the base commander, the highest ranking general on Fort Gordon, had been called in did not bode well for us. The fact that we weren't being smoked scared me even more.

So we waited. At one point the billowing smoke wafted towards our group. One dumb fuck started coughing and complaining.

"Maybe we should move over just a tad," he said. The first sergeant wheeled around and glared at him. We decided that it would be best to just breathe it in silence.

Eventually an SUV rolled up, and sure enough, a general and

command sergeant major emerged. We hit the position of attention. The general barely looked over at us as he conferred with our first sergeant and the fire chief. The fire chief then led them into the woods to show them what we'd done. We waited. I began to wonder who the scapegoat for all of this should be; my vote was and is still for Bryan—skinny little cunt.

Through the haze, the installation command team returned. They slowly walked before us and looked us over studiously. My clothes felt tight and sweaty.

"Men… you committed an act of arson on a military installation and have burnt a considerable amount of federally protected woodland." The general spoke sternly and loudly as he looked us over. I knew we were dead meat.

"But that treehouse and tomahawk throwing range were fucking cool," the general said, surprising everyone, though it probably wouldn't mean much in terms of the consequences of our actions and what our punishment might be.

"Gentleman, you fucked up, but damn if this isn't the best fucking thing that's ever happened on this installation," the general said. He turned to the 1SG. "These are the kind of warfighters that we need in the Signal Corps. Hooah!"

"Yup, try not to start any more fires though," the general warned us. Then just like that, they laughed and left. They walked off into their vehicle and drove off. Our first sergeant stood in front with his back turned towards us, eerily still.

We stood in silence for a while, even after the installation command team had left. We were all dumbfounded, and thought surely somehow, we were still getting fucked. It was obvious that our first sergeant was confounded as well. We waited for his response. He turned, looked us down, shook his head, and turned away again. Finally, he addressed us.

"You fucking shitheads. I can't believe this. But the command team does not want to press any charges, or have any administrative action be taken. I don't know how ya fucks are getting away with this… After class, report to my office."

"Roger that, First Sarn't," we all said in unison.

After class, the first sergeant was not at his office. Over the ensuing weeks, he said nothing to us, and as usual we tried to avoid him. Our cadre, naturally, had banned us from going into the woods and wanted us to hang out where we could be observed. This happened to be in the same area as some of the newer soldiers, which wound up backfiring on them, because a couple of our guys wound up fucking a couple of the trainees, and then we were suddenly given woodland privileges again.

Somehow, we got away with causing a forest fire on federal land, with zero consequences. I still can't believe it. Often, I wonder if life since then has been some sort of exhaustion-induced hallucination, and that I am in fact still being smoked.

GOAT FUCKER

This story occurred while in AIT at Fort Gordon.

It was Halloween eve, and I knew there was only one place to be—East Carolina University. I'd called all my buddies but only one had answered my call to action. I'd been driving for hours, heading all the way up to Fort Bragg to pick him up.

"Dude, I'm on Ft Bragg! Get your shit we're going to ECU!"

"Why?" he asked.

"Because they had a riot last year and everyone got tear gassed!"

It wasn't uncommon for my friends to receive these kinds of calls from me. Few of them could match my level of excitement. But luckily there was one idiot who was always down for whatever. Greg.

"Sure, dude, meet you out there in five," said Greg.

"Sick!" I said.

Greg implicitly understood that wherever crowds were getting tear gassed, there was a good party. Before I knew it, we were tearing off towards Greenville, North Carolina. Along the way we realized that costumes were in order. Luckily, I already had something in mind that I hoped would get me laid. We rummaged through a costume shop where we found a costume he liked, and I bought a black beard. But still my costume was incomplete. I dragged him through Walmart where I purchased camouflage pants, bandages, a black long-sleeve shirt and some white tape. But the most critical component of my costume was missing. I got on Google and typed in "life-sized goats near me." After some searching, I found our solution.

"Come on, Greg, we're going somewhere."

We entered the (to be unnamed) sex store, and I found my quarry. An inflatable goat sex toy. It was full-sized, complete with both goat vagina and anus. I proudly took it to the counter. Award-winning silence ensued as I pushed the inflatable sex goat box to the cashier.

"Do ya'll have an insurance policy on these?" I asked, trying to lighten the mood.

"No, we don't," the cashier said, and shot me what I thought was a judgmental look. I felt a bit awkward, and so did Greg.

"Look, lady, I'm putting a costume together. I think it's gonna get me laid, and if not… well, I'll have the goat," I said, laughing. The cashier did not respond. Greg slapped his forehead. I began to wonder if I had gone too far, though I would never admit it.

Dusk was coming, and we suited up. Greg dressed in his Uncle Sam outfit, while I prepared mine. I laced up my combat boots, tightened my belt over my camo pants, and donned the intimidating black turtleneck. Next, I wrapped bandages around my head, forming something resembling a turban. Adding the beard, I then proceeded to inflate the goat. On a side note, the designer thought it would be a good idea to place the rubber inflation doohickey right about where a goat penis would be. As I blew the goat (pun intended), Greg decided to weigh in.

"Did you buy a hermaphrodite sex goat?" he asked

"I don't think so, I think the inflatable bit is far too small. Though I'm no goat penis expert," I said.

"Hang on," Greg said, pulling out his phone.

"Check this out." He flipped his phone around to me, and I saw some sort of mountain goat licking its own penis. It was much longer than I expected.

"Okay, so this isn't a goat penis." I said.

"Definitely not a mountain goat penis." said Greg.

I continued blowing the goat, confident in my heterosexuality.

♦

We Ubered over to the downtown area. Right away, outside the first bar, were what I would estimate to be over a hundred cops, all in a huddle, probably discussing tonight's battle tactics. I knew shit was going to be legit.

We started off at a bar and got pretty hammered. Several patrons thought my costume was awesome, so they bought Greg and me a bunch of shots. At only nine p.m., I was loaded and dressed like a terrorist. We wound up making friends with a friendly banana and a gorilla. Perhaps we were overly friendly—their costumes were pretty suggestive in hindsight. Perhaps I'd misjudged their intentions with us.

At eleven thirty we decided it was time to make our way to a nightclub. En route, there was a group of Christian fundamentalists screaming at all the college-aged pedestrians.

"You are all sinners and will burn in hell!" one yelled.

"The end is near!" another shouted.

I walked up to them and stared them down, which gave them pause. I was a large man in ISIS battle regalia with an inflatable sex toy. I think I was a special combination of frightening and off-putting.

"Can we help you, sir?" one of them asked me nervously, offering me a pamphlet. By this point in the night, I was fully committed to my character. I'd even developed an accent that the banana had told me was spot on. It was some strange bastard child of Indian and Irish.

"Goowett that soppy infidel shite away from me, ya fuck!" I said, swatting the pamphlet away from me. This silenced the wannabe Westboro Baptists until a group of scantily clad girls lumbered by.

"You will burn in hell! Repent! Repent—" they said.

"Nrooo you da one be burnin' in the fiery ass crack of the Prophet Mohammed, praise be his name! Allah shall smite thee, infidel!" I screamed at the zealots.

"Repent, America is the new Sodom and Gomorrah! Repent!" they screamed.

"Death to America! ISIS shall turn the sea red with the blood of the infidels!" I screamed.

"Sir—this is our corn—"

"Allah Akbar!" I looked over at the Christian fundamentalists, who were now staring at me like I was the crazy person. A group of dudes walked by.

"Guys, when I say Allah! You say Akbar! One… two… three… Allah!"

"Akbar!" they said jovially. I laughed hysterically. Several groups of people started coming by at this time and taking pictures with me. A small crowd had developed and were very interested in our squabble. Cops even started to take notice. Greg, in his Uncle Sam costume, put me in a headlock. The crowd went wild. Just when I was about to turn this into a WWE super slam type of event, the radical Christians began packing up and left our area of the strip. We'd established dominance. People cheered for us. I lifted my goat in what would become my signature salute. Surprisingly, a group of girls came up to us.

"You're heroes. Those people are so obnoxious," drunk girl number one said.

"I love your costumes. What are you, a terrorist?" drunk girl number two said.

"Hell yeah, Jihad every day," I said.

"What is that you're holding, a lamb?" drunk girl number two asked.

"Sorta. It's a goat, and you're welcome to hold it," I said.

Drunk girl number two eagerly snatched the goat out of my hands and began inspecting it and prodding at the holes.

"Uhh, what's with these holes?" drunk girl number one asked. The other girl giggled.

"Oh, it's a sex doll, he's supposed to be a no-good Haji, goat fucker," said Greg in his Uncle Sam outfit.

"What's a hooji?" asked drunk girl number one.

"Oh, you know," said Greg, informatively, "a Bin Laden, camel-jockey, diaper head, derka derka?" he said, and still the girls drew a blank expression. "You know a dune coon, fig gobbler, shit hand, sun goblin?"

"That's so racist, patriotic Santa," drunk girl number two said.

"I know, right? Old Uncle Sam over here, no cultural sensitivity," I said, hoping they'd overlook my costume and my sex goat.

"You haven't fucked this thing, have you?" drunk girl number one asked.

"Not yet, and I won't have to if things go my way," I said, with what I hoped was a charming smile. Drunk girl number two laughed, but drunk girl number one did not.

"He'll fuck it, though, if you don't fuck him!" Greg said.

"Ladies, this is not a hostage situation," I clarified.

"Go home with him or the *goat gets it!*" Greg said. There was no recovering from this, so I wished the ladies a good night, then Greg and I headed towards the nearest club.

It turned out we'd fucked around on the corner with the fundamentalist for far too long. There was a line around the block to get into what was apparently the only bumping club. Seeing as we were just two dudes, I knew that the odds of us getting in were quite low. I spotted a VIP line and quickly devised a plan.

"Greg, follow my lead." I confidently walked by the whole line, and pushed my way to the front of the VIP line. There two large bouncers looked at me incredulously.

"Are you guys on the list?" said the particularly hench-looking one.

"We're with the goat," I said, pointing to my goat sex doll. This made both of the bouncers laugh. Much to my delight, they let both Greg and me in without any further questions.

Now I was feeling fucking invincible. In this costume, with this goat, I could do no wrong. I began aggressively hitting on chicks.

"Allah promised me virgins, but I'll settle for you!"

"Do you want to pet my goat?"

"How about you, me, and the goat later?"

"Death to America?"

This went surprisingly well. Once I had gotten several girls to write their numbers on my goat, I got real cocky and decided that the party wasn't hype enough. I stood on the DJ's stand and yelled, "Death to America!" before it was popular, and threw my goat into the crowd, where it crowd-surfed, like a fucking rockstar. The goat was a huge hit, and everyone in the club wanted to hold it. It was bounced around like an inflatable ball at a concert. I was the life of the party and loving it.

Then the bouncers got involved. These professional buzzkills ripped the goat out of some girl's hand, then threw it into solitary (a fenced-off area behind the DJ). I was incensed. Like Hannibal from the A-team, I devised a rescue operation.

I knew that I couldn't be the one to save the goat. I was far too high profile (a VIP after all) so I recruited a group of girls dressed as slutty football players.

I explained the situation to them, then gave them their orders. Two of them would flirt with the DJ, while two others stood by to run interference with the bouncers, while one of them secured the hostage.

I watched from afar as my Charlie's Angels conducted the operation. It was a nail-biting affair. I didn't know if my goat was going to make it out alive.

The mission was a success. The slutty football players returned the package intact like they were Delta Force.

The crowd went wild.

A bouncer tapped on my shoulder, then proceeded to escort me and Greg off the premises.

It was the end of our night, and as we were drunk and poor, we passed out in the back of our car, with our goat, as one does.

♦

The next morning, early as fuck, I dropped Greg off at Fort Bragg and made the long drive to Georgia to show up at my unit hung over but in time for the battalion "Halloween Run." Here the battalion so cleverly tried to boost morale by making us continue to show up at 0530 and run five miles. This time though they made it "fun" by allowing us to come in costume. Not all of us did, because some of us were intelligent and concerned about becoming a heat casualty—I was not one of these people. I showed up to my battalion in my ISIS costume, complete with turban, combat garb, and sex goat in tow. I was still a little hammered from the night before, and perhaps my judgment wasn't as good as it should've been. However, luckily for me, my company commander and first sergeant saw the costume and asked me, "What the fuck are you supposed to be?"

"I'm an ISIS goatfucker, first sergeant." Luckily ol' first sausage was an Enduring Freedom vet, and had stacked many bodies.

He thought it was hilarious. "Let me see that goat."

I handed over my inflatable goat and had to stifle my own laughter as he turned it around and discovered the plastic goat vagina. He looked from the goat vagina, back to me, then back to the goat vagina. "Is this a sex toy?" he asked me. His face grew stern, and I felt scared. But not too scared to crack a dad joke.

"She's a very baaaaaad girl, first sergeant."

He immediately dropped the sex toy, disgustedly. "Specialist... did you fuck that thing?!"

"Not yet, first sergeant..." I said.

"First a forest fire, now this," 1SG said, before walking off. I think he secretly loved it.

Shortly thereafter I got moved to the front of the formation, with the goat in hand. We took off on a run with a cadre running alongside, leading the cadence. Eventually they started swapping us in and out. I wound up to the side, and I began a "death to America cadence," which the soldiers in formation chanted in a very spirited manner. To this day I still don't know how the battalion commander felt about this. But the first sergeant seemed to be laughing, which was either a good sign or a really really bad one. I ran back into formation, towards the front, and handed the goat off to a nearby runner. He lifted it up likes it was the Olympic

Torch, and screamed, "Hooah!" The goat was then handed off to a bunch of others who were clamoring for their turn to lift up the goat… the newly appointed mascot of our "fun run." Truth be told, this was the most fun I have ever had during a "fun run."

Until tragedy struck.

Someone passed the goat onto another soldier, who held it up high. And just as he lifted it above his head in triumph, the goat popped. The air leaked out of it, and it deflated before my eyes. As the air hissed out of it, I felt pangs of sadness. Though I didn't know it yet, an epoch was coming to an end. The blissful simplicity of my early days in the Army would fade away, muddled and dirtied by the failures, pain, and the hard-learned lessons that were to come. Along with the air leaked out the last bastion of the carefree spirit that encompassed this age.

The laughter, excitement, and sense of adventure have become but faint echoes. With that sex goat, died my innocence, my naivety and childlike sense of wonder. My life would be very different. Much more serious, as the hardship of life, war and death would lay heavily upon me. I would reminisce about the old carefree days as a young soldier. When we were still full of hope, had bright futures, and were free and unencumbered.

Just kidding, I remained an asshole idiot. Now I was just without a goat sex doll. If there is a moral to this story, it is this: never take for granted your time with that special someone. You never know when they might pop on a battalion fun run.

SOF VS LARPERS

I tend to easily bore, and when I get bored, I look for things to do. I was still in the 82nd at this time. It was a Thursday leading up to a four-day weekend, and unfortunately, I did not have any plans. I was quickly looking for a way to remedy that issue, so I went online, through the great rabbit hole of modern life, and I found one of those group meet websites where people with very particular or unusual interests organized events. I'd read on some forum that these meetup groups were a fantastic way to meet chicks and get laid, so I found a couple.

I was skeptical, but willing to give anything a shot. I found poetry groups, drag show groups, even pole dancing classes, which I eagerly applied to (but was turned down due to being a dude). Nothing was catching my interest until I came across an ad for a Medieval Sword Fighting Club. Clicking on the link took me to their website. It had pictures and videos of dudes in full armor, beating the Christ-fuck out of each other with swords. Right away I knew that this would be a panty dropper. I would literally be a knight in shining armor.

It looked incredibly dope, and the website said that newcomers could sign a waiver and get involved in a sparring session. Better yet, there was a meetup that night. Quickly, I clicked the link and bought three tickets. Now all I had to do was find two people who would be dumb enough to come with me.

Enter Austin and Stewart, two Special Forces candidates whom I'd been friends with since basic training. Austin was your regular good ol' Texas boy meathead. Christian, Republican, Black, and a bit of an introvert who rarely left his room. In fact, come to think of it, in all of my years of knowing him, I never once stepped foot inside his barracks room. I wonder what he was hiding in there? Probably some weird anime shit, I would guess.

"Yo, Austin, I've got tickets to go to a medieval sword fighting class. Wanna come with?" I said.

"Hmmm…. What does this class entail?" he said in typical Austin style.

"Uhhh, swords and fighting with them," I said.

"Interesting, but you know, I've got a pint of Blue Bell in my freezer, so I think I'm gonna pass," he said. My brain went into hyperdrive, concocting my next sales spiel.

"Come on you pussy, you afraid I'm gonna whup your ass in sword fighting? Like I did in racquetball?" I said. Austin was still sore about losing; I'd been on something of a winning streak.

"You would have no chance against me," he said.

"You said the same thing about racquetball, yet here you are, zero wins and five losses," I said. He stayed silent for a while.

"Austi—" I said.

"I'll be ready in ten, you pussy," and he hung up. I fist pumped; that was one chump down, one to go. I called Stewart.

"Do you want to go to a medieval sword fighting class with me tonight?" I said.

"Yes, I would like that," he said. I was startled that he agreed so easily. I had a whole sales pitch ready for him.

"Sweet, see you in the parking lot in ten minutes."

A short while later, we were in my Honda (yes, still driving the same old Civic), driving to Raleigh, N.C., to the address that the medieval sword fighting website and group meet website had posted.

During the drive, some startling revelations were had. One, we learned that Stewart had been a collegiate fencer, which blew our minds. Also, Stewart had a website that served as a personal diary, listing his accomplishments, travails, and emotional journey through life. Austin and I eagerly went through the website and began forwarding it to all our friends. Stewart had layers like an onion—the more you peeled back, the weirder shit got.

After about an hour of driving, we closed in on the location. The GPS guided us into what appeared to be a park of some sort. I double checked the website and confirmed that I had in fact put in the address correctly. We followed the GPS, and it took us to the playground. "You have arrived at your destination," it chirped. We looked around and didn't see a building, or anything that looked like a medieval battleground. Then we spotted a very small group of people underneath a community overhang, swinging plastic swords around.

"Oh, that must be them," Stewart said. I turned off the car, and we approached the group. As we approached, the group, which had been engaged in some sort of animated discussion, halted, and they all glanced at us or at the ground nervously. I surveyed the group, and surmised that the fat man in a leotard, with a ponytail and greasy skin, was probably their leader. I approached the alpha cautiously.

"Excuse me, we're here for the Medieval Sword Fighting Class," I said. The alpha, who stood about eight inches shorter than me, scoffed, leaning against his sword and sizing us up.

"Well, this is the place. Have you brought signed waivers?" he said. I proffered three signed waivers. He looked them over and back at us, as if he were trying to match our signatures to our faces.

"Well, now that I have these, I must forewarn you that this is a physically rigorous class. There will be physical exercise, and if you can't keep up, you're welcome to leave," he said derisively. Austin pulled off his Pit Vipers, seeming annoyed by the comment from the puny alpha.

"I think we will be just fine," I said, finding this terribly amusing.

"Okay, so come over here and grab your swords." He gestured towards a rack of swords. Austin and I eagerly grabbed some plastic swords and began swinging them around like baseball bats. While Stewart appraised a sword or two and seemed to be checking their balance. Then we moved into the line with the rest of the students, who seemed to be all in their mid-thirties, and who also seemed to favor leggings and other tight clothing, and probably still lived in their mother's basement.

"Ladies and gentlemen, in order to become a sword fighter, you must be physically fit; fitness, endurance, and grace are what separates a skilled bladesman from a dead one," the alpha said. He glanced haughtily at the three of us.

"Now everyone, do high knees," he said. He began rapidly pumping his knees into the air; his belly flopped around, and his ponytail swung wildly. After about thirty seconds the instructor called a stop, panting heavily. He glanced over at the three of us, none of whom had even begun to sweat. Little did he know that we were all soldiers and were accustomed to running twelve plus miles with eighty pounds strapped to our backs.

"Now everyone, drop down and give me ten!" the alpha said. Ten? I looked at my comrades and we shared a mischievous grin. The alpha banged out about five or six before his arms began to shake hard. From what I saw, amongst his people, he might indeed be the strongest, as the others faltered somewhere around five. He was not happy when he saw that Austin, Stewart and I were easily able to bang out ten, not computing that we literally got paid to do push-ups.

"Alright, alright, that's enough of that," the alpha said, having to pause to catch his breath. He was not even looking at us at this point.

"Next, we shall move on to positions and defensive work," he said, dropping a foot back and moving his blade into a blocking position. Now he was in his element; the alpha looked at us again with a sneer. He knew he had us; finally, he could reassert himself as the dominant alpha male, and try to bang the one twenty-seven-year-old Asian girl with transition lenses and braces.

To his dismay (and Austin's and my surprise), Stewart was lithe and agile with his blade, striking positions and poses with great balance and dexterity. But the instructor would not be shown up.

"No! No! You're doing it all wrong! You want to hold it like this," he said, and tried to reposition Stewart's hand. Stewart wasn't having it.

"No, I think I'll keep holding it like this," Stewart said.

"No, you won't, not if you want to *live*," the instructor said, raising his voice.

Now he had the attention of the entire class. All eyes were on him and Stewart. Austin was behind me. "This is gonna be awesome," he said.

"No," Stewart responded, "this is definitely better." The words hung in the air like a challenge that the instructor now had to meet to save face.

"Well, I guess you should be the instructor then. I've only spent fifteen years in competitions across the region and learning from legends of the sport."

"Hmm, then why don't you show me why my block won't work." Stewart took a step back and put the sword up challengingly. The instructor couldn't refuse. The students backed away, and now the mock conflict had everyone's rapt attention. The instructor lifted his plastic blade.

"I will punish you for this insolence," he said, assuming the character, as though this were an actual battle. And to him, it was. He took a quick step and made an overhead right shoulder attack. Stewart parried and quickly stabbed the instructor in the gut before moving quickly back out of range of the instructor. Clearly baffled, and now red-faced with anger (and probably embarrassment), the instructor lunged in again for a second attack. This time, Stewart, while moving backwards, smacked the instructor's hand hard with his blade before going in for two quick stabs, and then moving back out of range once again.

"Oh, so someone's a fencer! I can tell you that wouldn't work because real swords are heavy and I'd be wearing armor, so you just fucked up and would be dead a million times," the instructor said.

"Do you have any real swords?" Stewart asked seriously. The instructor laughed.

"You better be thanking your lucky stars that we don't have any real swords," the instructor said. This seemed good enough for the other students, and we resumed training. But the alpha of medieval sword fighting had clearly lost his mojo and his confidence. Stewart had taken that from him, and as a final fuck you, Stewart asked the brace-faced, transition-lensed girl for her number, and got it, right in front of him.

Stewart had established dominance. Unsurprisingly, we were not thanked for coming out. On our way walking out, two ten-year-old kids on bicycles rode past and screamed "losers" at the group of sword fighters.

"Come here and sword fight me, you little bitch," said the instructor. The kids laughed at him and pedaled off.

"Come here and sword fight me, you little bitch" would become our catchphrase for the next couple of weeks.

A BUBBLE BATH

This story occurred while in special operations.
 It'd been a long day of saving elephants and shit. As a gesture of gratitude, the conservancy's owner gave us our pick of lodgings that were conspicuously vacant due to the uptick in poaching.
 I chose a wooden cottage situated on a hillside, in a secluded spot next to some fig trees. It overlooked the river and the sweeping vistas that teemed with life; the cottage was replete with a brick patio and outdoor tub, and inside a king-sized bed was situated behind panoramic windows.
 The sun was setting behind the golden savannah. The hills and animals who wandered the vast plain cast long shadows. I was awestruck, and knew that under normal circumstances, I could never afford to come here on an enlisted man's salary. I decided to take advantage of every amenity offered while I could.
 As dusk came, I lit the torches and the fireplace and filled the bath. Earlier I'd taken advantage of the open bar back at the lodge, downing several glasses of scotch and then maintaining my buzz with Tusker Premiums. I was relaxed and eager to soak my sore body in the lavender-scented bubble bath.
 Night came as the last of the sun's rays dipped below the horizon and disappeared into the distance, leaving only a faint glow that soon melted away. I found myself in a bathtub staring up at the starry sky. The night sky was more vivid out in the savannah, where there were no city lights, cars lights, or house lights to

muddy the clear atmosphere; the air was clean, the altitude was high, and the only light came from the fire that I had lit. Where the nighttime soundtrack in North America is a quartet, the African savannah can be likened unto an orchestra: the winds susurrate the trees and grass, the insects pluck and fiddle, avian creatures cluck, click, and hoot, and the fauna accent the melody with irregular bleats, snorts, and roars. It was a symphony that had been perfected over eons.

It was magical.

It was shaping up to be a very romantic evening with myself until monkeys in the fig tree beside me began to scream.

Earlier, over a glass of scotch, the hosts had told me that monkeys had three different types of warning screams, each signaling a different kind of danger. There was one for snakes, one for eagles, and one for lions. It is believed that our primitive ancestors shared this alert system, and that the mythological chimera known as the "dragon" is simply the amalgamation of this primitive fear: a lion's head on a serpent's body with an eagle's wings.

I lifted my head, alerted, listening to them hoot frantically, trying to gauge what predator it was that they had identified. My skin burst out in goosebumps, the hair on the back of my neck went erect, and adrenaline sent blood to my extremities. The brush nearby began rustling; I heard deep, sonorous breaths. A musty, powerful odor wafted toward me. My deep primitive brain knew that something feline was nearby. Now that my inebriated brain was cognizant of the situation, I began to panic. My mouth became dry and my heart raced. My stomach felt queasy as blood diverted away from it, and my fingertips throbbed with each pulsation.

I sloshed around in my bathtub. Everything I knew about fight or flight told me that if I did not move to release the extra oxygen that was building up, I might become lightheaded. Suddenly I heard the brush move more around me, and a low growl vibrated in the stillness of the savannah. I froze. If I hadn't already shit myself earlier that day, I would probably would have done it again, right there in the bathtub.

I held still and tried to assess my situation, keenly aware that I was being watched. Though unsure of what was out there, something deep in my bones was telling me it was a lion. I'd been near them before, during the day when they are docile, and I recognized the scent. I knew that I probably shouldn't try to beat them in a footrace to my screen door. My vision became more acute, and I tried to see into the shadows.

Tribal leaders I had worked with had told us stories of "Simba" (Swahili for lion) murdering villagers and livestock, warning us to not go outside at night. The brush around the terrace and cabin wasn't especially long, but I'd seen for myself how easily a huge lion could disappear into the golden grasses. It was only about five yards between me and my screened cottage door, but I was not confident that I could make it that far. If I hopped out of the bathtub and bolted for the cabin, they'd get me. I couldn't see it, or them, but I had no doubt they were keenly aware of my every move. I bravely cowered in the lavender-scented bubble bath, next to the fire.

Earlier that day, I'd seen a female lion feasting on a kill. I remembered her sitting on her back legs, ripping out chunks of flesh with quick snaps of her neck. My teammates marveled at the fact that just her neck was powerful enough to move a two thousand pound Cape buffalo carcass across the ground. For perspective, her neck muscles were able to exert at least double the force of the human record for deadlifting. Not to mention that they have excellent night vision, superb hearing, with ears that acted like megaphones and were able to twitch to better capture sound, an incredible sense of smell due to the size of their nasal cavity, and swift, agile feline reflexes, with claws and teeth that could disembowel a man with a single blow.

I knew I was pretty fucked and began to regret my decision to take a bubble bath outside in the savannah. At least I had a lit fire next to me; hopefully that would keep the monsters at bay.

The monkeys were screaming wildly now. Then I heard another low growl, followed by a heavy, raspy breathing. The lion was very close. I began seriously considering the possibility that this simba might maul me to death. From what I'd seen on the Discovery channel, it seemed like it would be neither a quick nor painless experience. I wondered if the hosts would find a bathtub full of blood in the morning. I probably would make the front page of the local news. I wondered what conclusion my teammates would come to, how much shit people back at home would talk, and whether in future safety briefings they would explicitly tell soldiers, "Do not take bubble baths out in the African savannah!" I would die a grisly death, and my only legacy would be extra-long safety briefings. Sad, I'd really hoped to have a greater impact in the world. I just hoped that my life insurance company would pay my fiancée out.

(20 minutes later...)

The bath water was beginning to cool, and most of the bubbles had popped. Worse yet, I had fed the fire my last logs, so it was dimming. It seemed to me that the lion was encroaching towards the retreating light. I realized that these lions weren't going anywhere and waiting them out was no longer feasible. I had to get to the cabin. The question was, how? I deliberated throwing something to try to distract the lions, but I didn't have much. I considered grabbing a log and holding it like a torch, Rambo style, but like an idiot, I'd already committed all of them to the fire.

I did have some bottles of Tusker nearby, and I had an idea. In a Liam Neeson movie trailer I'd seen, he'd fought a pack of wolves off with broken glass he'd duct-taped to his knuckles. I did not have duct tape, but I did have empty beer bottles, two of which I broke. I held the broken bottle necks like they were knives. Another I threw into the woods, where I heard it shatter. I slowly stepped out of the bathtub with my two broken beer bottles, careful not to make any sudden moves, held them out in front of me, and faced the direction where I reckoned the breathing was coming from. I tried to make noises and sound tough, growling and snapping my teeth. This might not have been the best idea in hindsight. Isn't baring of teeth considered an act of war in the animal kingdom? I even did a Tarzan yell. Yes, I did. I don't know if this worked, or if perhaps the lions were just surprised to see a naked Mzungu with bubbles dripping off him.

I slowly backed up the path that led towards the screen door of my cabin. I heard a rustle to my right, and whipped to face the threat, giving whatever lurked in the darkness full frontal nudity. I retreated further, away from the dying light of my fire.

Good, at least now I can die like a man on my own two feet, I thought. In hindsight, I'm not sure if the headline: "Special Operations Soldier Killed by Lion After a Bubble Bath" would've been much better. At least my pale, bloodied, organless corpse would be easy for the search party to spot.

With these thoughts swirling in my mind, I traversed the most terrifying five yards I'd ever moved in my life. I reached for the flimsy screen door and shut it behind me.

It seemed hardly safe enough to house royalty. But I supposed during normal conditions that this facility would house more people, and there was safety in numbers. Unfortunately, as of that moment, there was only me and a bunch of empty huts around, hence the lions were bold enough to move in. I began lighting the lanterns and placing them in front of the doors, hoping that these meager flames would keep the beasts outside at bay.

It goes without saying that as I laid in my bed behind a mosquito net, I did not sleep well. I was hypervigilant all night, roused repeatedly by hollering monkeys and the deep breaths of lions just outside the walls.

The next day, I learned two interesting things.

First, Liam Neeson died at the end of that movie, so smashing the Tuskers was probably a bad idea. Second, that there had been a couple of African wildcats spotted in the camp, which are similar to your regular house cat. It's possible that I overreacted.

RAWR

This story occurred when I was a Special Forces candidate.

I'd met a girl on Tinder named Sarah. We went on a date, which led to another date.

When I arrived outside her apartment building, she was there waiting for me in the parking lot.

"Hey, what's going on?" I said.

"Oh, just so excited for you and Finch to finally meet!" she said. I remembered that she had a German shepherd that she loved and swore up and down was the sweetest and bestest dog to ever live.

"Oh... yeah, you know, I'm pretty excited too," I said, feeling not even a little excited.

I followed her upstairs to her apartment. She made me wait outside while she went in. I heard the dog sniff the door and give a very low and audible growl. I felt a lump in my throat. She moved him to the other room and invited me in. Nervously, I came inside, and she brought me over to the kitchen island and gave me a couple of doggie biscuits.

"Oh, I just know the two of you are going to be best friends. Here... just give him these treats and tell him he's a good boy."

"Uh, is he in..." I heard low snarling and smashing coming from behind what was presumably the bedroom door.

"This is... great. I'm really looking forward to this."

She went to the door, and I mentally prepared for war. "Okay, here he comes." She opened the door, and from the dark room emerged a large black German shepherd with his ears pinned back and hackles raised. He stalked towards me, fangs fully displayed. I stepped back.

"Easy there, boy... easy... hey, here's a treat for the good boy." I held a treat towards him. Finch's dark eyes flashed between the treat and me; cautiously, he approached, snatched the treat from my hand and backed up a few steps. I offered him another treat. Again, he approached cautiously, and quickly snagged the treat out of my hand. He snarled and growled again, but his hackles were lowering and he seemed visibly less on edge. I was winning him over. I felt like Kevin Costner in *Dances with Wolves*.

"That's a good boy, Finch," I said, and handed him another treat, and another. Before I knew it, I was petting him and he was eating out of my hand, literally.

"Aww, looks like you have a new best friend," Sarah said.

"Yeah, I think we're good now. You can just start calling me the Dog Whisperer." As I said that, out of the corner of my eye, I saw a flash of fur. Time seemed to slow as Finch leapt through the air, mouth open, baring his fangs. He committed, and he was going straight for the family jewels. I managed to take just half a step back before his fangs closed down on the crotch of my sweatpants.

Finch latched on. I began spinning and fighting the dog for control of my pants. "Finch! Finch! No!" I was swinging the dog around, trying to get him to let go.

"Oh, he's just a bit nervous is all. Finch, it's okay, boy!" Sarah said.

While she was reassuring me how he was really such a sweetheart, I was battling for my life and the lives of my future generations.

"Finch! *Nooo*!" I yelled.

"Rawwwwrrr," Finch said. Finch began tossing his head and pulling at my sweatpants. My pants were ripping, and I was concerned about the proximity of his teeth to my scrotum. I began a furious tug of war with the dog, trying to dislodge him.

"Sarah, *open the door*!"

"What?" she said. She probably couldn't hear me over the snarls of her beloved baby boy.

"*The door to the fucking bedroom! Open it!*" He was pulling hard now, nearly knocking me off balance, and Sarah was not responding hurriedly. I was trying to calm the dog down, restraining myself from punching him and gouging out his eyes. I still wanted to get laid, after all. She opened the door, and I was able to swing him in through the door and punch him in the face without Sarah seeing. He released, and I slammed the door shut on him. He growled and jumped at the door from the other side, shaking it. I backed away from the door, panting. I looked down and saw a couple of holes and tears from where he had latched on. Then I panicked.

I quickly pulled my pants down and began to examine my balls. I duck-walked with my testicles in hand to the kitchen table—I could see them better under the light. Sarah stood to the side, staring at me. I realized both that my balls and penis were perfectly intact, and that this was the first time she was seeing my penis and balls. It was not the best showing. They'd gotten a bit scared by the tussle and had turtled their way back up inside my abdomen, which I promptly explained to Sarah. She really didn't have anything to say on the matter.

A little while later, she let him back into the living room. We mingled, and things seemed to be better. I think my punch let him know who was boss. He wouldn't even make eye contact with me. I even managed to get an arm around Sarah without him even batting an eye. We were finally cool with each other.

As the evening progressed, things got a bit spicier, and Sarah wanted us to move to the bedroom. We did and began to get things going. We'd closed the door behind and left Finch in the living room. Just as things were getting good, I heard a loud pounding on the door. Sarah lifted her head up.

"Oh, that's Finch. He likes to be able to see me. I'm just going to let him in real quick!" She began to get up

"I don't think that's such good idea!" I said.

"It'll be fine. You had your little spat, now you're good!" she insisted.

"Sarah, let's leave him outside until we're done at least," I said, but my compelling logic was ignored and in came the big black dog. Quickly, he dashed onto the bed and lay in the spot where Sarah had just been. He was looking at me, and my very exposed, erect penis. I felt a lump in my throat. I was beginning to think about putting my clothes back on and leaving, but Sarah shooed him off the bed, got back into position, and we resumed clapping cheeks.

I was pounding her from behind and beginning to forget that the dog was even in the room with us. That is, until he positioned himself to the side of the bed right where I could see him. He was making strong eye contact with me and snarling. I didn't break eye contact with the dog the whole time I railed his mom from behind. He did not look happy about it. I feared that if I broke eye contact he would strike, and that if I stopped fucking, that he would perceive it as a form of submission, neither of which I could tolerate. I kept banging his mom until he broke eye contact, whimpered, and went off into a corner. It seemed that I'd won this battle at least.

Eventually, we switched positions. She got on top of me. I was lying on the bed, things were going great, and I no longer was having a stare down with an angry German shepherd. Then I felt hot breath on my feet and a low growl. I couldn't see him but knew he was about to strike.

"Finch! No!"

"Yeah, baby, you like that!" Sarah said.

"No, you psycho! Finch! No!" I threw Sarah to the side and got up to shoo the evil creature away. Sure enough, he was there with his dripping fangs fully exposed about to rip my foot off. I guess I hadn't subdued him with my glare, and that he was ready for round two, which on some level I respected, but mostly found very annoying.

"Oh, come here, Finch!" Sarah said and patted a spot on the bed next to her. She pet him, then spread her legs and gestured for me to continue. I did, despite there being a very angry dog now on the bed with us. I continued with nothing but an occasional growl and bristle from Finch.

◆

A week or two went by. Slowly, Finch stopped attacking me whenever I entered the premises. Incrementally, we got to a point where I could enter the house, approach and fuck Sarah, and not get attacked by him. I was beginning to feel like Cesar Milan himself. Things were going so well that Sarah suggested that I take him on a walk around the apartments by myself.

I looked at her incredulously. "Are you sure that's a good idea?"

"Yeah, you two are doing really well together," she said. I could tell that she'd put a lot of thought into this, so I leashed up Finch for a walk, feeling slightly manipulated.

Things went surprisingly well. He pulled on the leash a little bit. I told him no, and he seemed to respect my command. We were walking, he didn't pee on any fire hydrants, didn't chase after cats, nothing. I cleaned up a poop with one of those baggies. Everything was great. But it was jarring in a way that I can't really explain. This was serious boyfriend stuff, and I wasn't feeling that. I was starting to feel like breaking up with Sarah. Truthfully, I'd been thinking about it for a while, but the timing just had never felt right to me. Now I had a sense, for some reason, that it was the right time.

Being the introspective guy that I am, I had been trying to figure out why I'd started dating her in the first place, and why was I now just suddenly so okay with breaking up with her.

I'd done a few Google searches, trying to see if there was anyone else out there that could relate. I found a forum about guys being attracted to fixer-upper girls, and staying around until the job was complete. Thinking about Sarah, sure she was a little weird, but there wasn't anything that I felt was worth fixing. In fact, going back through any of my other relationships, I realized that this tendency to want to "fix" had never been a feeling I'd had.

In that moment, I realized that I wanted to fix her dog, her stupid, evil, fucking dog. I felt a weird responsibility to do it. Now, finally, it seemed that the dog was more fit for society, and that my work was done. I turned Finch around, set on breaking up with his mother.

I was feeling good, loose, and my swagger was coming back. As we walked, some young dudes on skateboards were coming our way on the other side of the parking lot. I was about to hit them with a White-guy head nod when Finch pulled the leash taught. I nearly fell to my ass before I realized that Finch was roaring and snapping at the skateboarders. I planted both feet and pulled.

"Finch! No!" But Finch didn't give a fuck; he pulled harder and was lunging at them like a hellhound.

"Sorry about that!" I said to the skateboarders as they rolled by me, giving me a the WTF look. I reeled Finch back in and he stopped bristling as I sweet-talked him. I wondered what had gotten into him. Perhaps he sensed my intention to leave. My heart was broken—he was attached. Me and this dog had something special going on.

That was until he lunged at a baby in a stroller. "Rah! Rah-wwwr! Rtawhhw!" Finch said. He was trying to snap at the baby. The scared mother wheeled her baby off down a curb and pushed her child away to safety at a trot. The baby began crying. I felt terrible.

"Finch! *No!*" I yelled and jerked the dog to the far side of the parking lot. This dog had turned back into a monster. I half expected his eyes to begin glowing red and rolling back in their sockets. "What the fuck is the matter with you!" I said. I looked at him and decided it was perhaps things with wheels that were making him angry. We still had a daunting quarter mile to go. I exercised caution and kept him off the sidewalk, pulling the leash tight when bicycles approached. For whatever reason, the bicycle did not set him off; he stayed by my side and barely gave the bicyclists a glance. We neared the building, passing by a number of people and wheeled objects without provoking a reaction. Now I just had to break up with Sarah.

I ruminated over this until finally I'd composed the most merciful and gentle breakup speech that I could imagine. What I'd invented was elegant and no nonsense. I had always felt that it was important to be upfront. Really, it made it easier for both parties. Settled, I approached the building feeling confident. Then Finch yanked me off my feet, trying to eat a dude with a man bun.

"Finch!"

After five long minutes, I eventually got Finch back under control, and returned to the apartment room. I was out of breath, but frankly feeling pretty good about all the people and babies I'd saved from Finch. If only the people out there had known that it was my girlfriend's dog, and I was a fucking saint. I was catching my breath and a bit thrown off by the last-minute fight for another man's life I'd had against Finch.

"Yo, Sarah, what the fuck is wrong with your dog?"

"What do you mean! He's perfect!" she said.

"Perfect? You serious? He just tried to kill a baby!" I said. I expected her to ask me for an explanation, as if this was some kind of unusual event, which would convince me that he was in fact just feeding off my vibe. The hypothesis was disproven, though, when she responded, "Oh yeah... sorry about that... I forgot to mention, he's got a few quirks," she said, pointing her fingers to emphasize how small these alleged quirks were.

"Quirks like he fucking wants to kill babies?" I said.

"Yeah, he doesn't like babies nor..."

"Let me fucking guess"—I interrupted—"guys with man buns, skateboarders, the crippled?" I said.

"I've never seen him go after a cripple... just dudes in wheelchairs," she said.

I slapped my forehead in genuine disbelief. "Sarah… where the fuck did you get him from? Like was he abused or something?"

"Well, no, my ex was a dog handler, and he gave me Finch right before we broke up," she said. Before I could psychoanalyze the dog and gain insight into his daddy issues, she provided me with more information.

"Oh, yeah, my ex told me that Finch, well, he was called Sergeant Cerberus before I got him, had been kicked out of the Army."

Cerberus was a very fucking appropriate name for him, I thought. But I had more questions. "Wait a minute. Finch or Sergeant Cerberus got kicked out of the Army? What did he do? Fuck a junior enlisted soldier?"

"No. My ex said that he was too aggressive," she said.

My jaw dropped. "Too aggressive. For the Army? They literally train their dogs to kill people. How the fuck was he too aggressive?" I said.

"Well, he would attack indiscriminately."

"And your ex gave him to you as a pet?"

"Well, he's on Prozac now!" She was getting defensive.

"Well, apparently you need to up the dose. Jesus Christ, that dog is not fit for civilized society," I said.

"Well maybe he's just stressed cause you're here, and he has to watch you bang me!"

"You're the one that insisted that we let him in and watch," I said. I shook my head. Now was the time. I needed to rip the Band-Aid off. I gave her the speech I'd so carefully prepared. "Look Sarah," I began. "It's not me, it's you. I think you're weird. We're breaking up. Your dog sucks. Deuces!"

It felt like I had lifted a weight off my shoulders. I turned and walked out the door. Halfway down the stairs I realized that I'd forgotten my jacket and wallet. "Shit," I muttered, and walked back up the stairs, and knocked on the door. On the other side, Finch answered with a low growl. "Sarah!"

That growl turned into a snarl. "I'm not letting you in… you asshole."

I could tell she was ugly crying by the mucusy sniffles. "Sarah…" I considered my next words carefully. I needed to get back into her apartment and retrieve my CAC—Common Access Card—if I lost it, I'd get in a lot of trouble with my command. I did the only thing that I knew would work.

I un-brokeup with her.

"Really, you mean it?" she asked.

"Of course, baby," I said. I heard her telling Finch to get back, and the locks began to be undone. She opened the door and let me in. Naturally, she was expecting a makeup make-out session. Now I didn't intend for this to happen. But one thing led to another. We went into her bedroom, we banged, Finch watched. Once we were done, I put my clothes back on, got up, got my jacket and wallet with all identifications accounted for, and walked out the door and to my car.

Courteously, I sent her a text. "For real though. I am breaking up with you." I hit send, blocked her phone number and all of her social media profiles, and changed my name to make it a little harder to contact me.

In hindsight, I recognize that I was, perhaps, a bit of a dick. However, that doesn't make me heartless. Sometimes I wonder how Finch is doing and whether he wound up in doggy jail, or if he ever ate one of Sarah's subsequent boyfriends. As much as I hate him, I feel for the dog. In fact, I see a little of myself in him. He's just a salty, frustrated, GWOT veteran, and an honorary member of the Department of Degenerates.

ABOUT THE AUTHOR

Alexander Lee is a combat veteran and former Special Operations professional whose writing draws from real-world experience and a deep interest in philosophy, artificial intelligence, and human psychology. An avid outdoorsman, traveler, and photographer, he crafts stories that explore the human condition and life's existential mysteries. With a deep respect for military culture, Alexander views Department of Degenerates as a celebration of the humor and camaraderie that define the lighter side of military life.

DEPARTMENT OF DEGENERATES WILL RETURN

———————————————

www.mindgame-manuscripts.com

www.ingramcontent.com/pod-product-compliance
Lightning Source LLC
Chambersburg PA
CBHW072154070526
44585CB00015B/1135